CASTLES

COLORING BOOK FOR KIDS

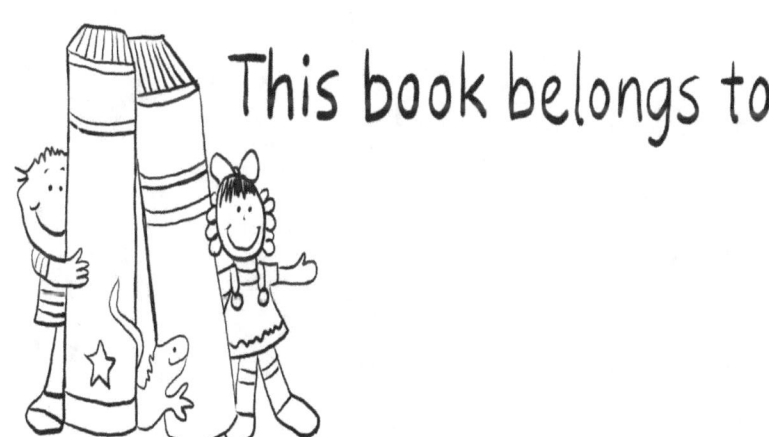 This book belongs to

Extraordinary Publishing

Visit our author page for more books:
Amazon.com/author/extraordinary

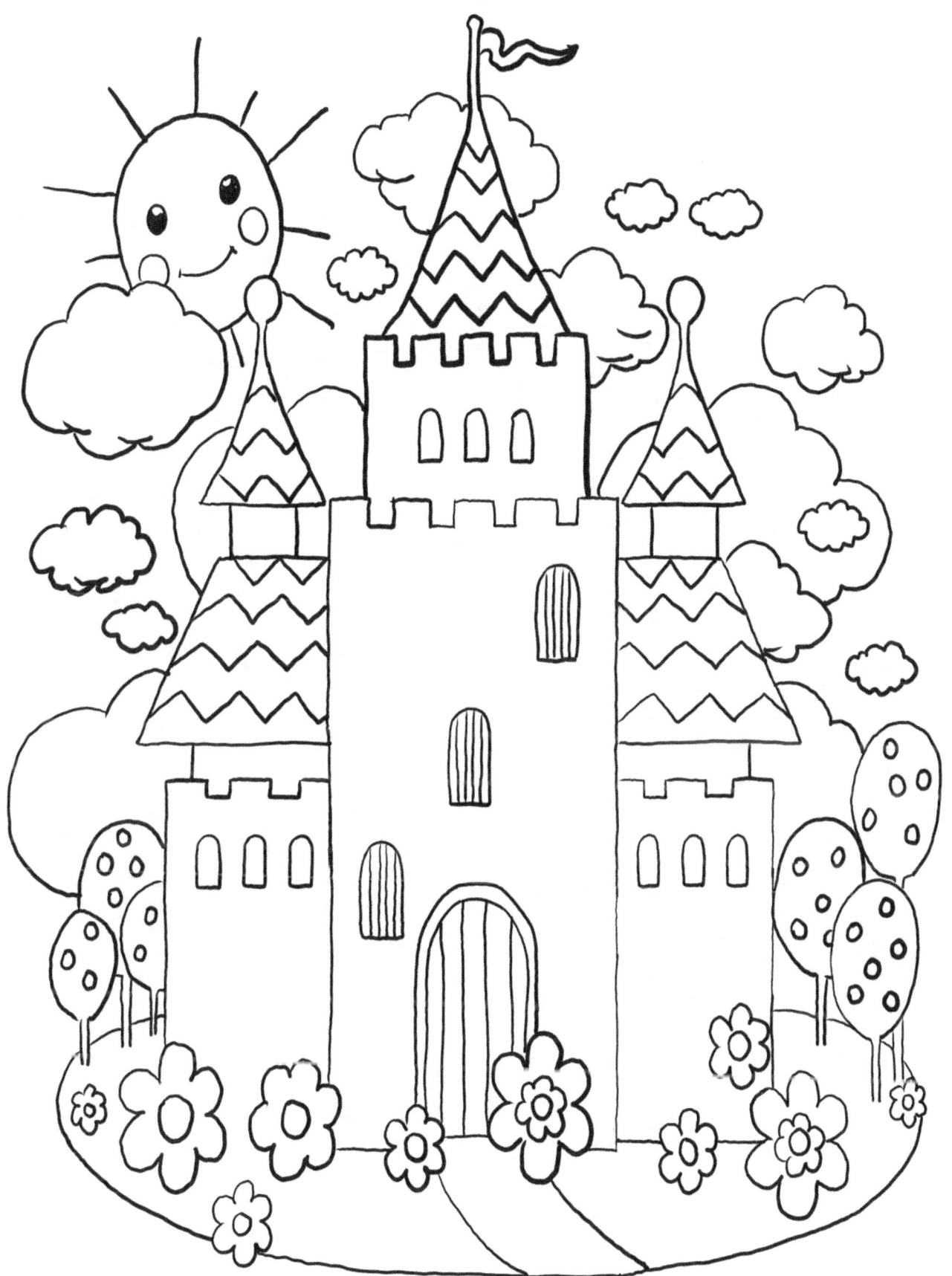

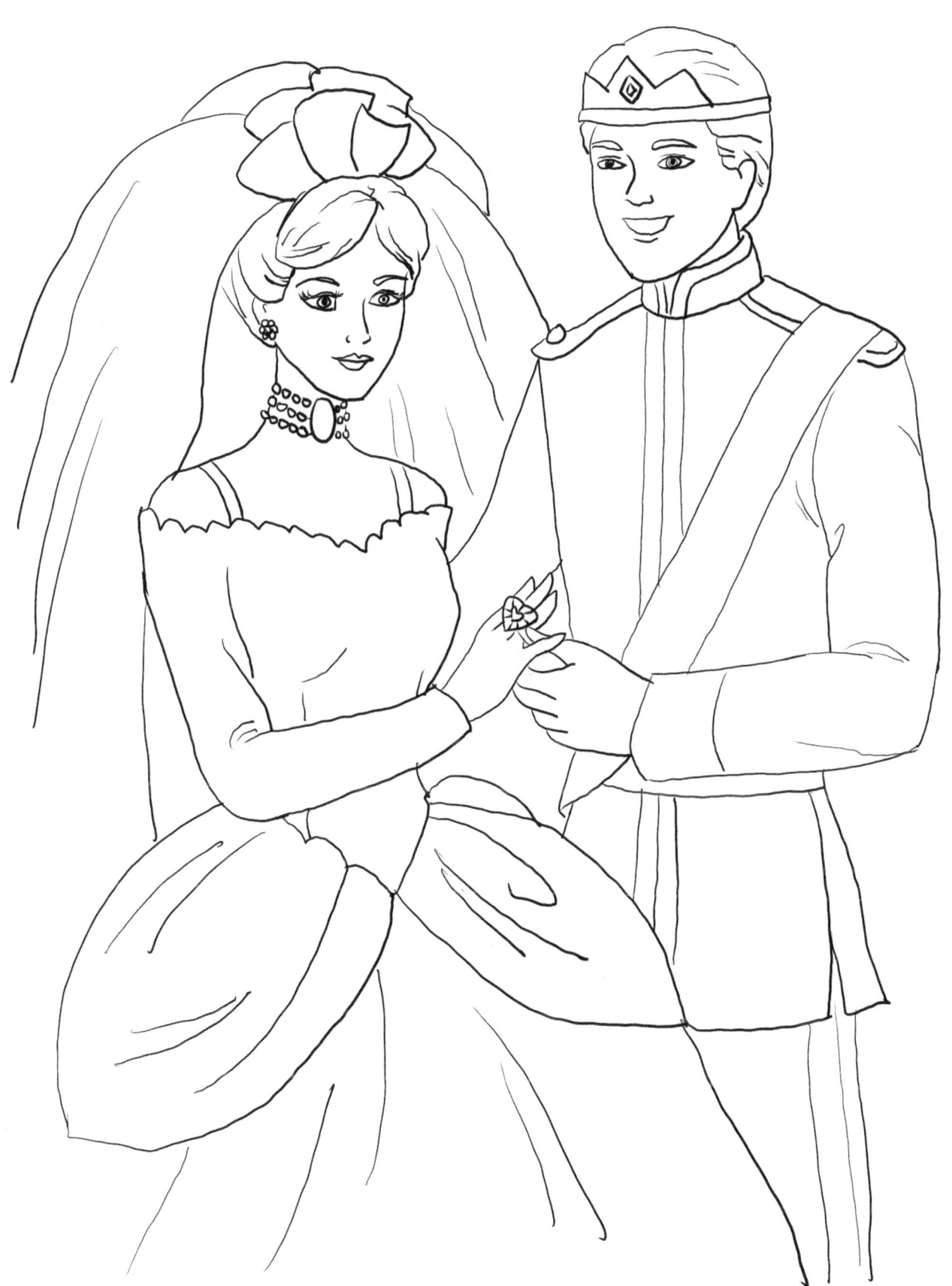

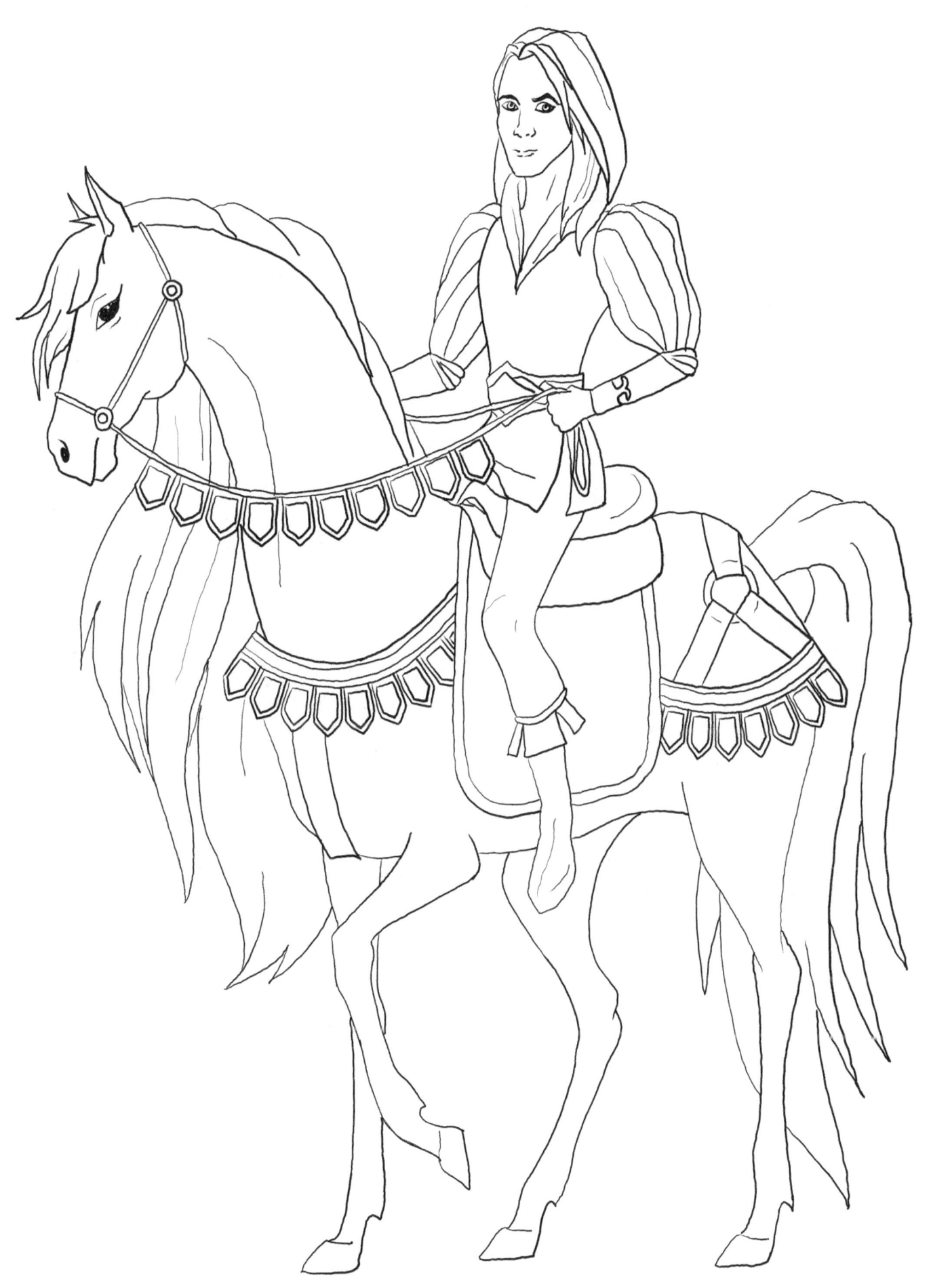

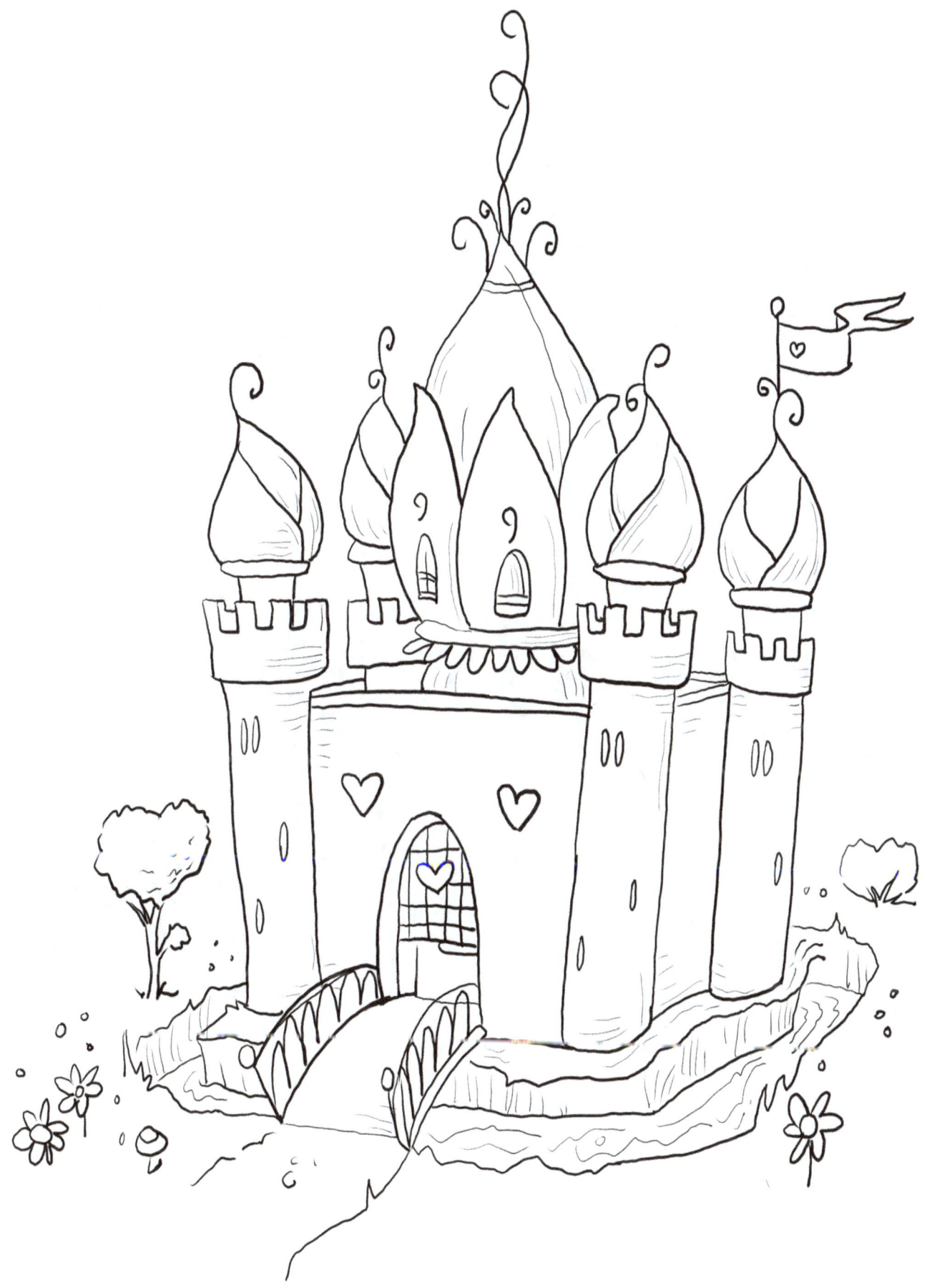

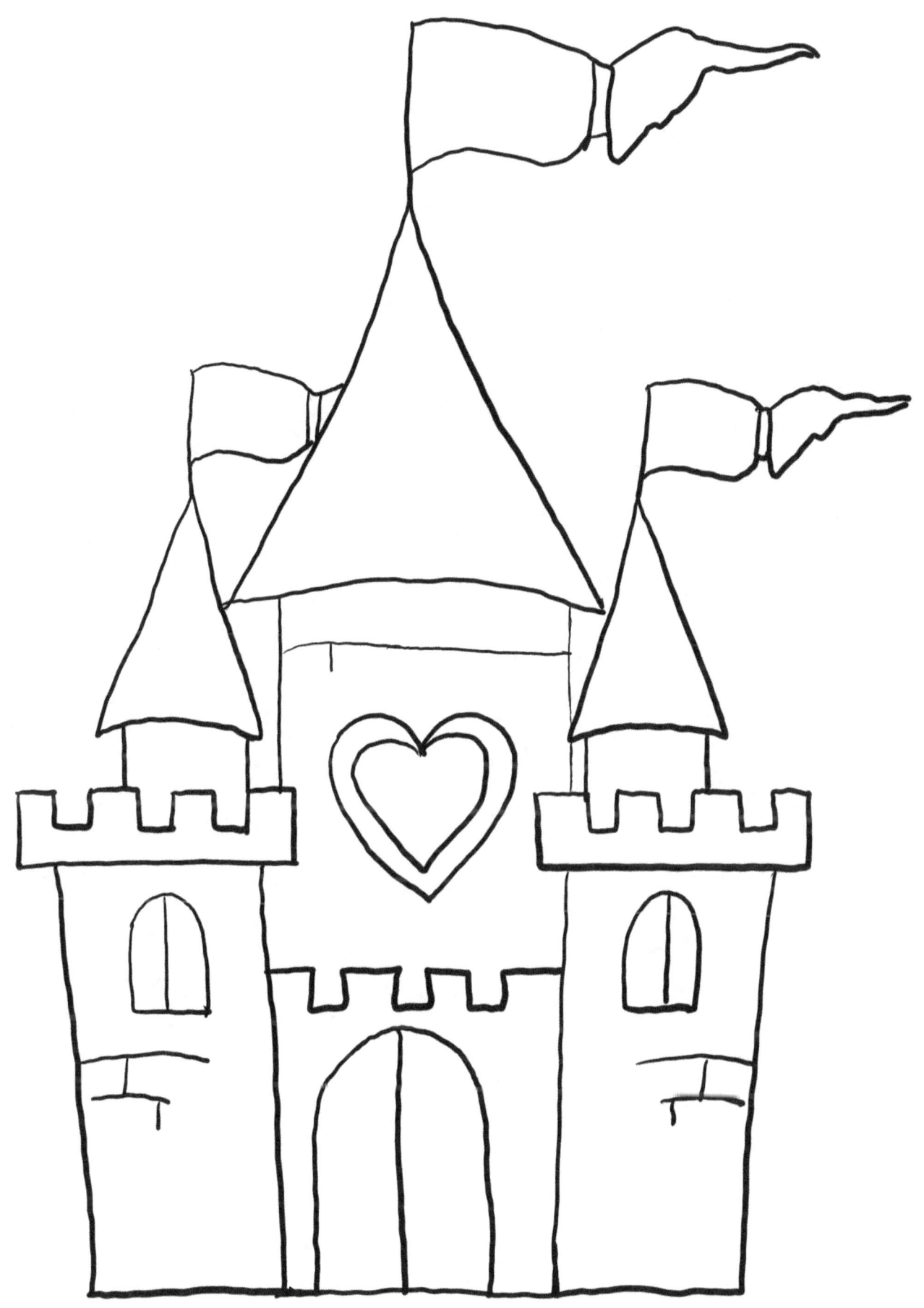

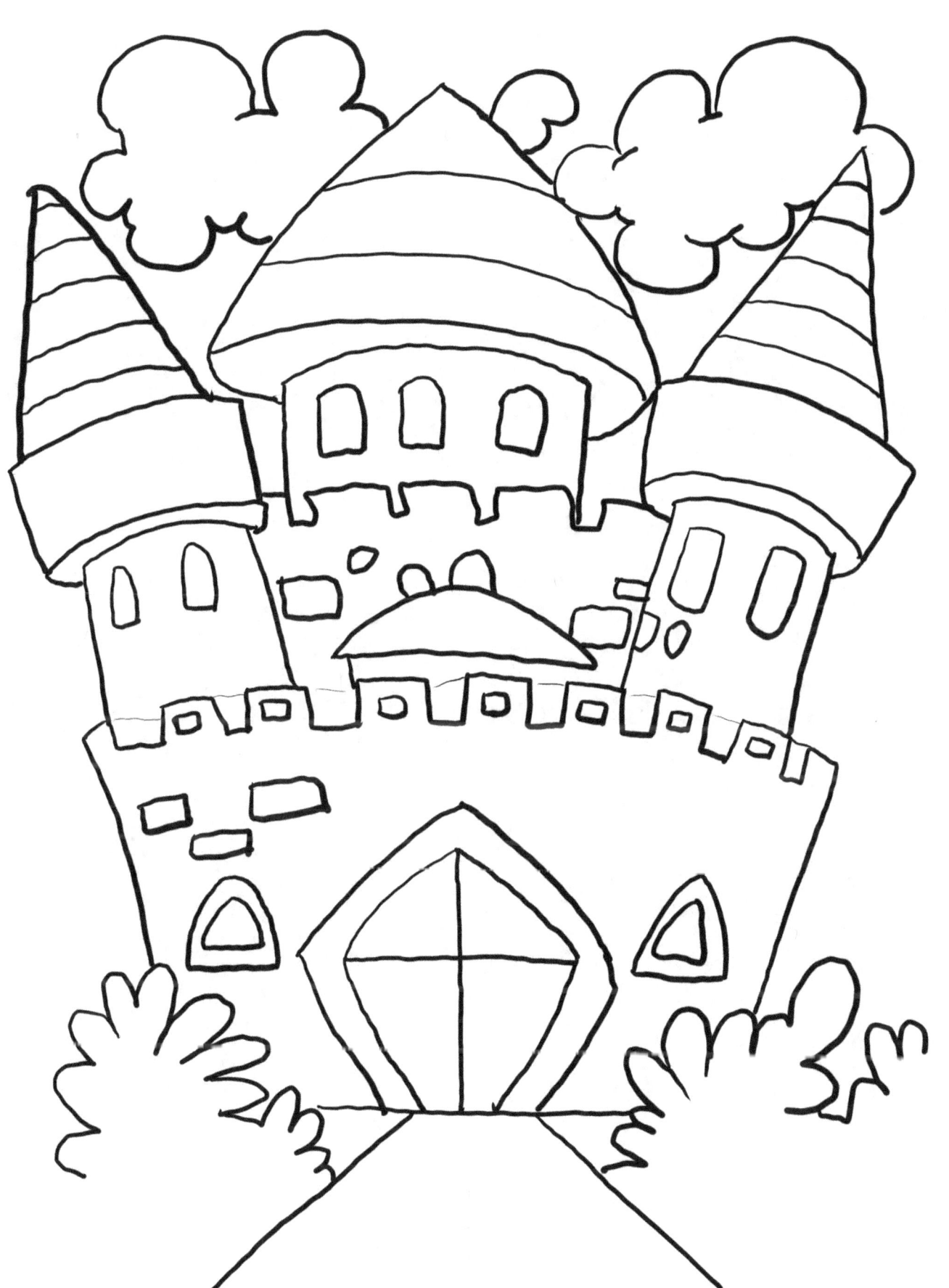

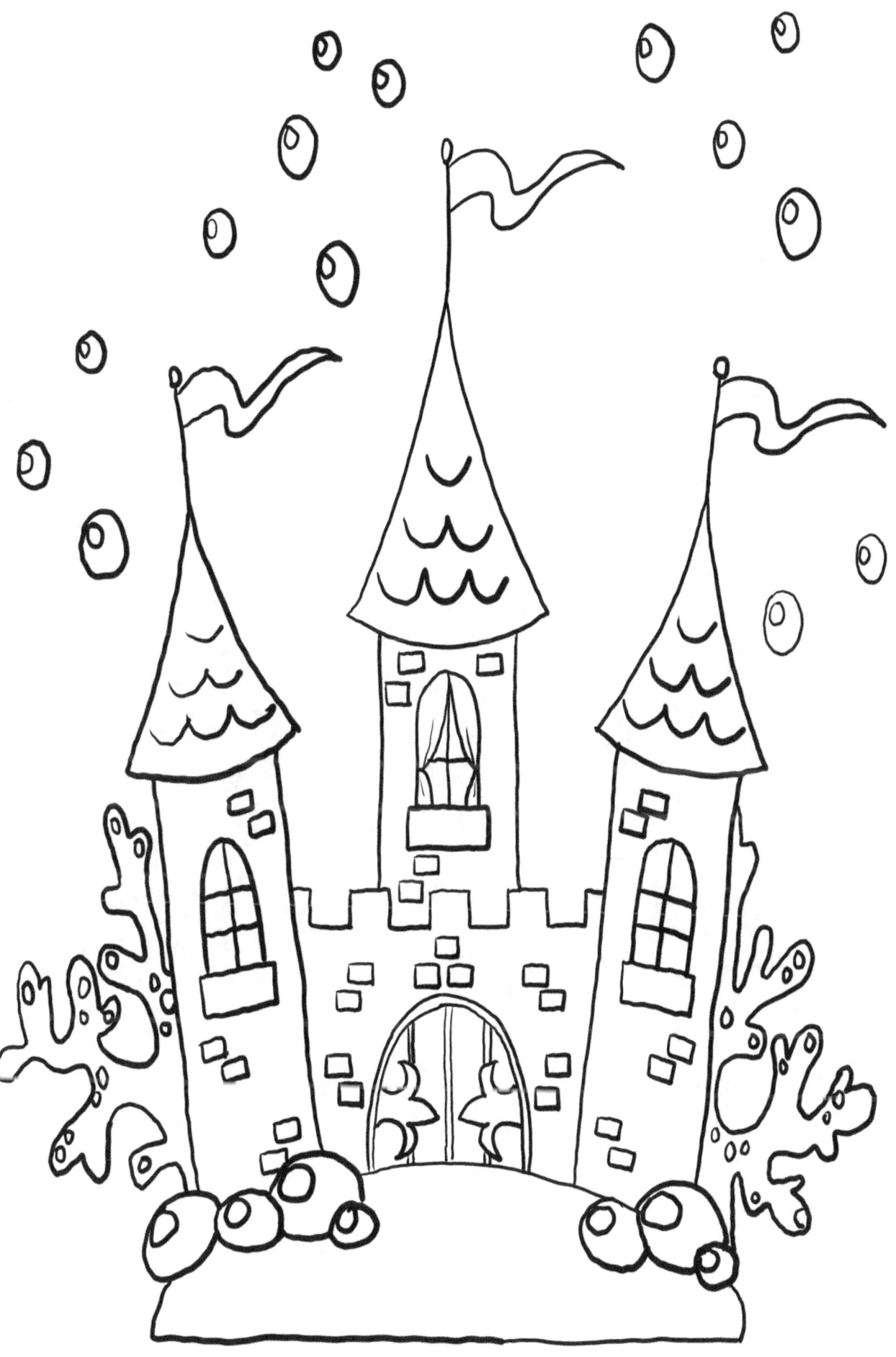

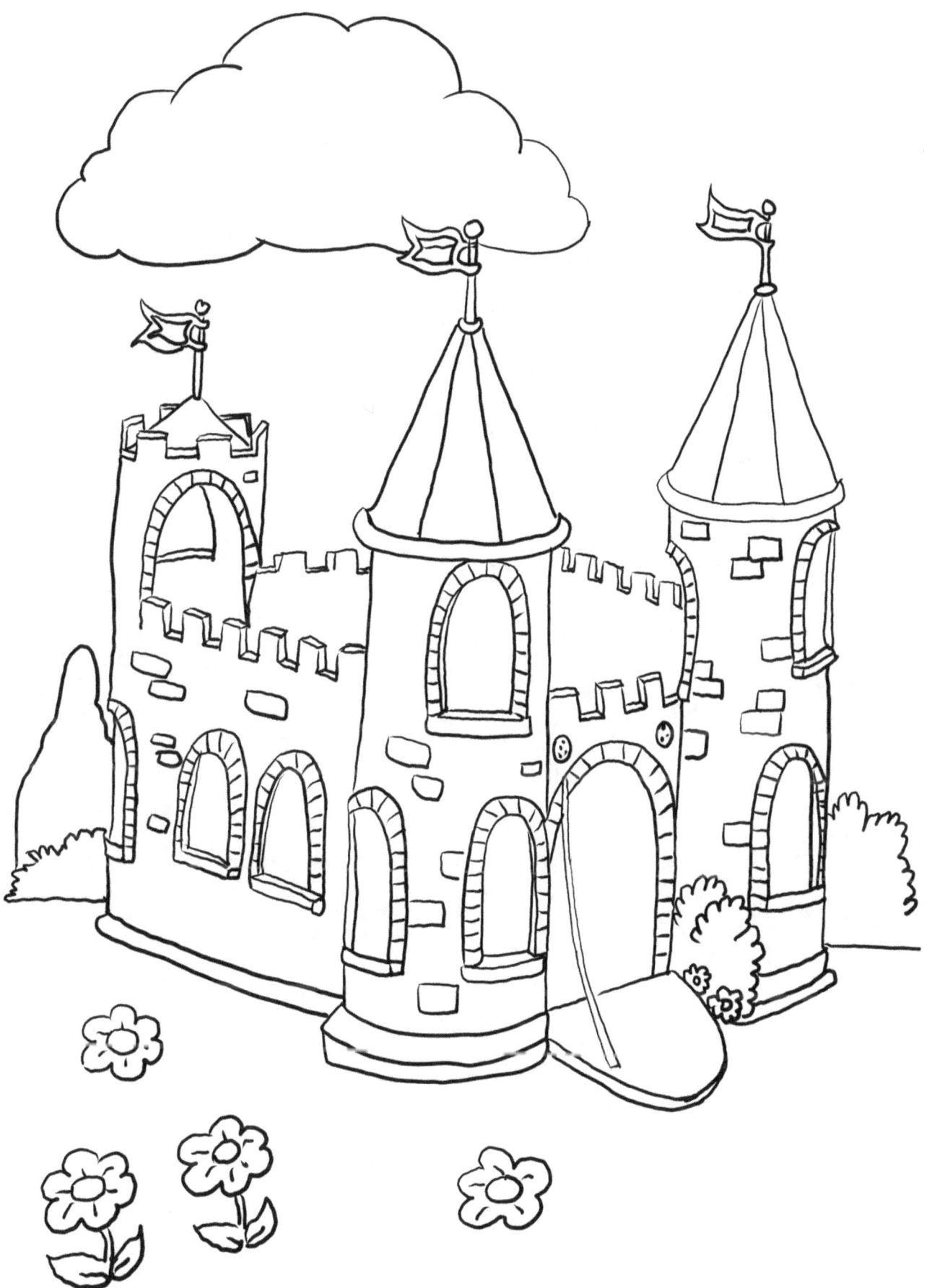

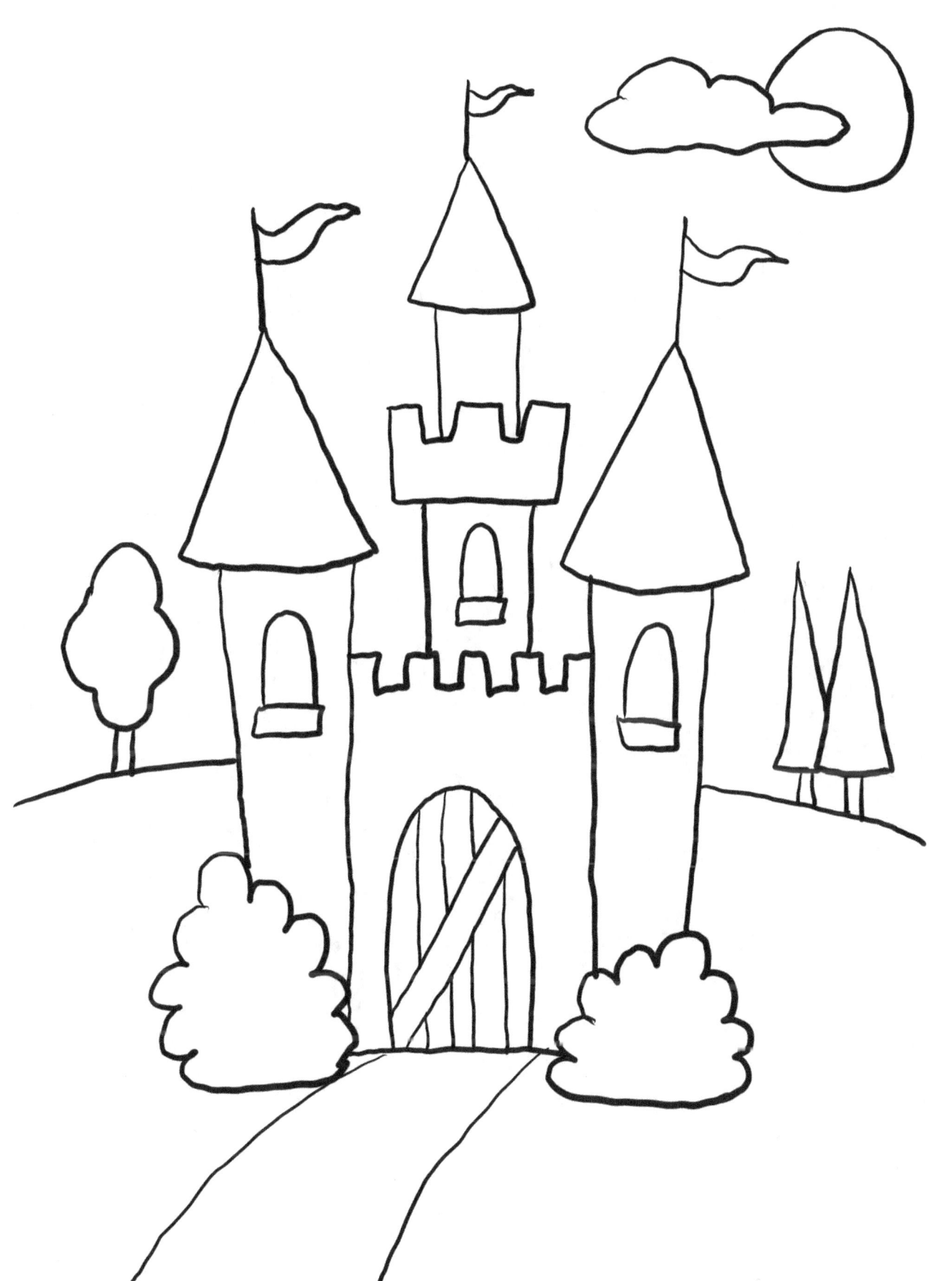

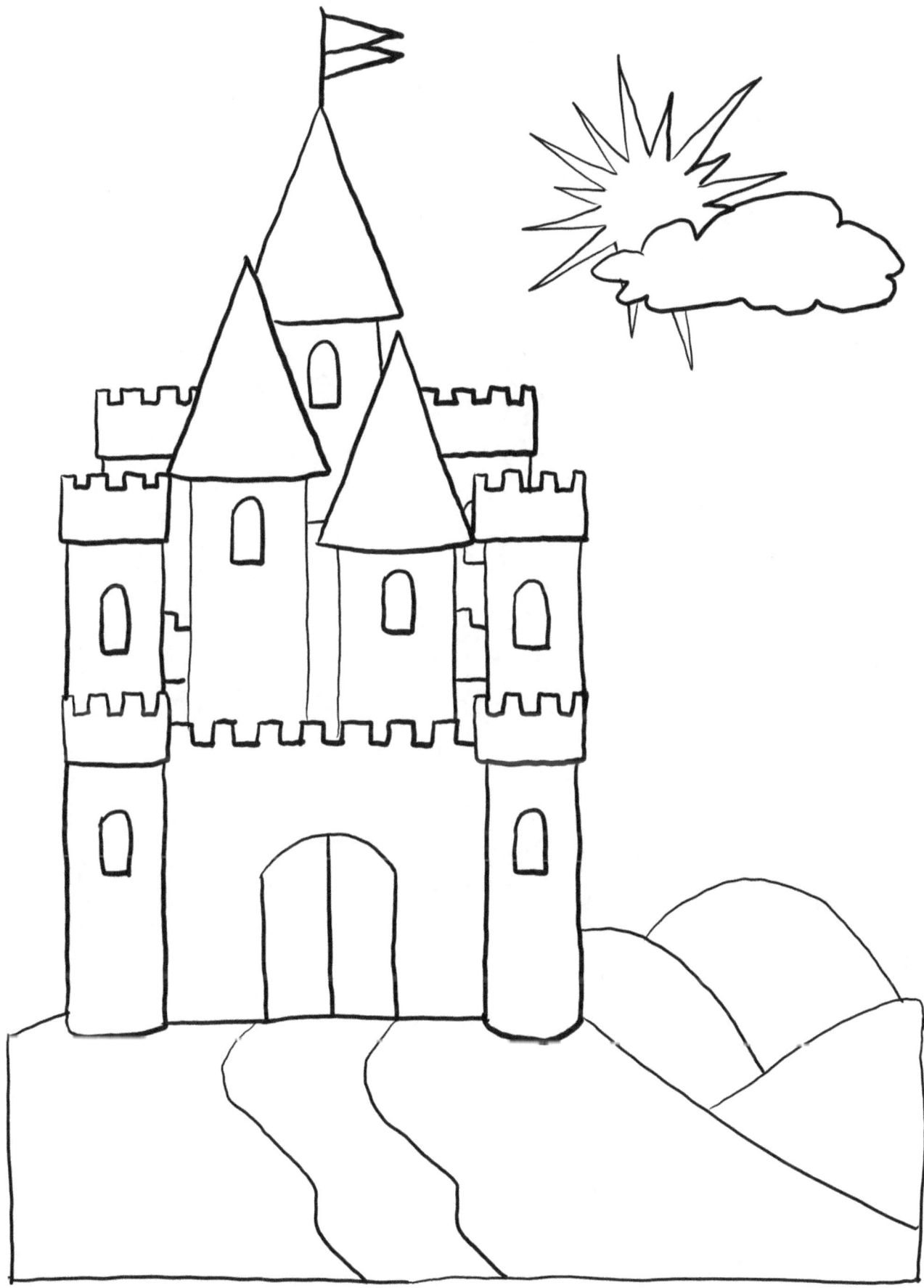

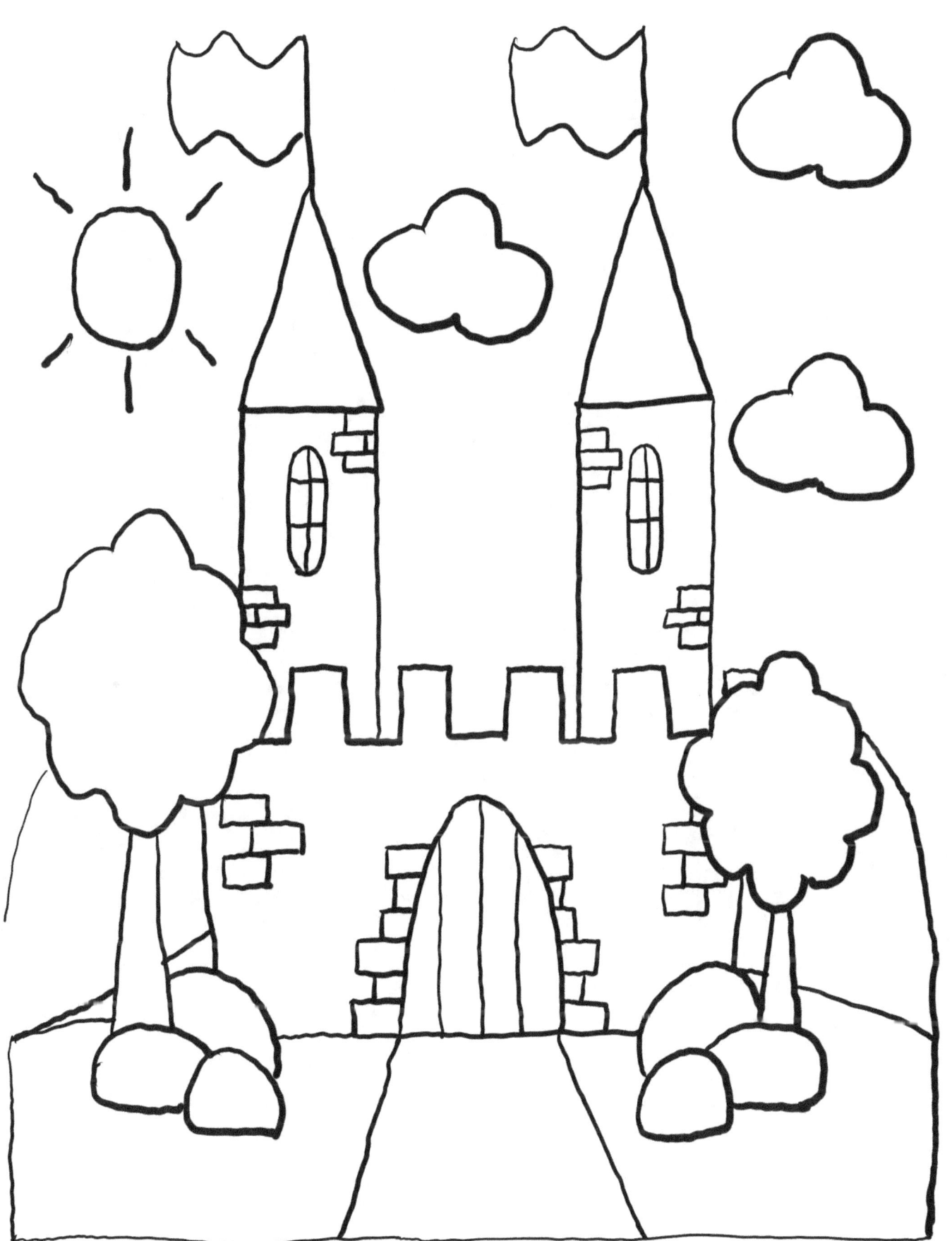

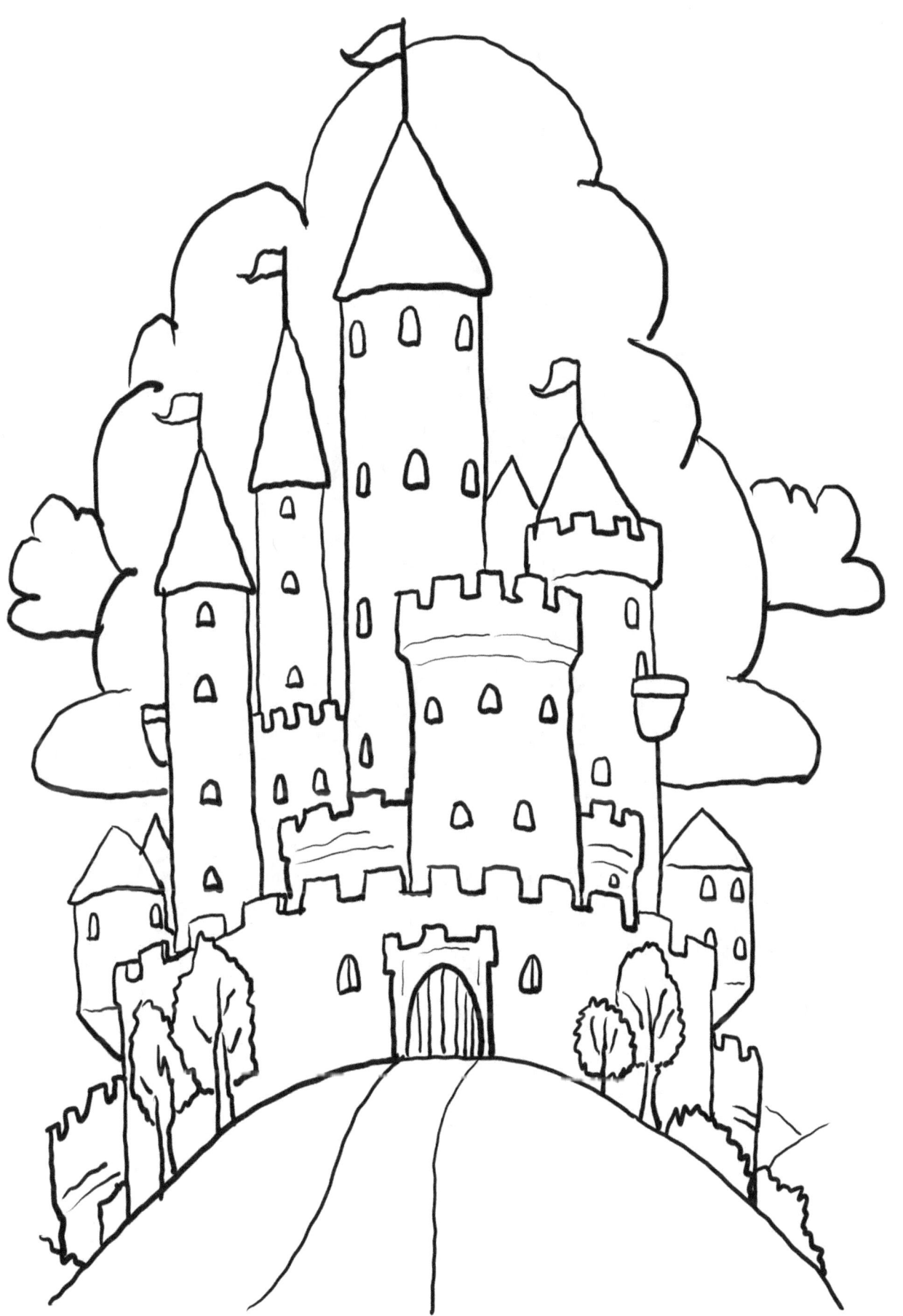

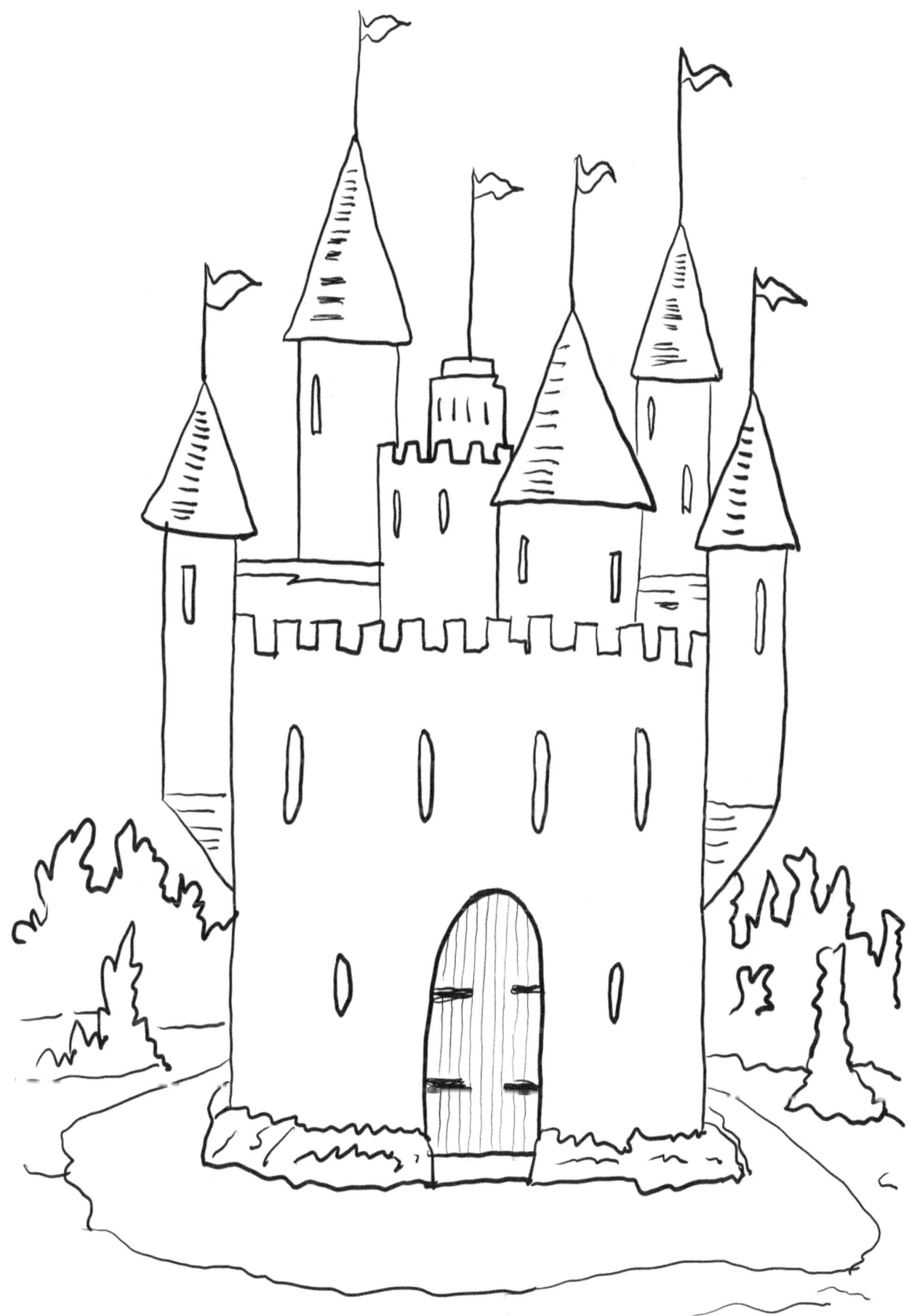

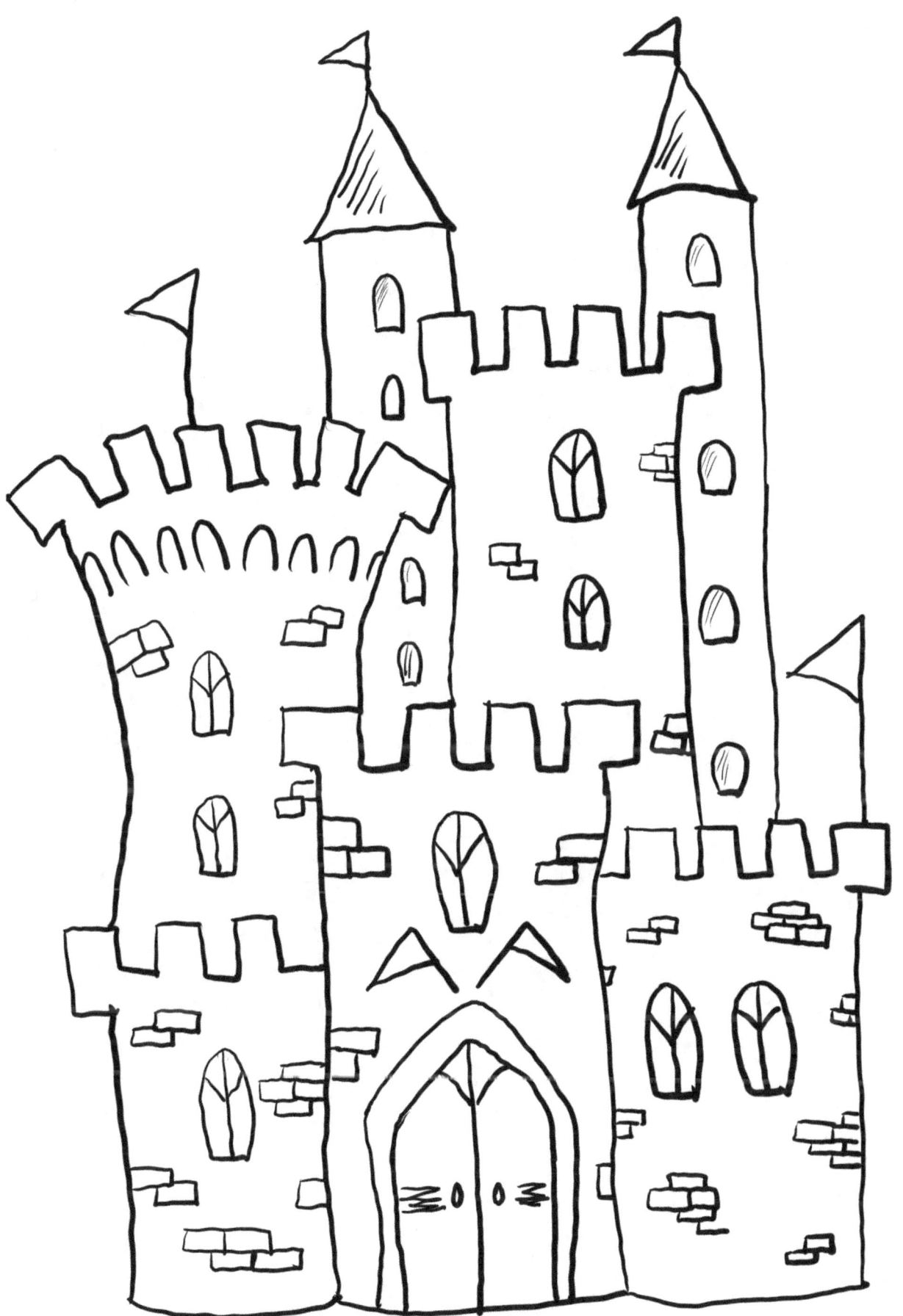

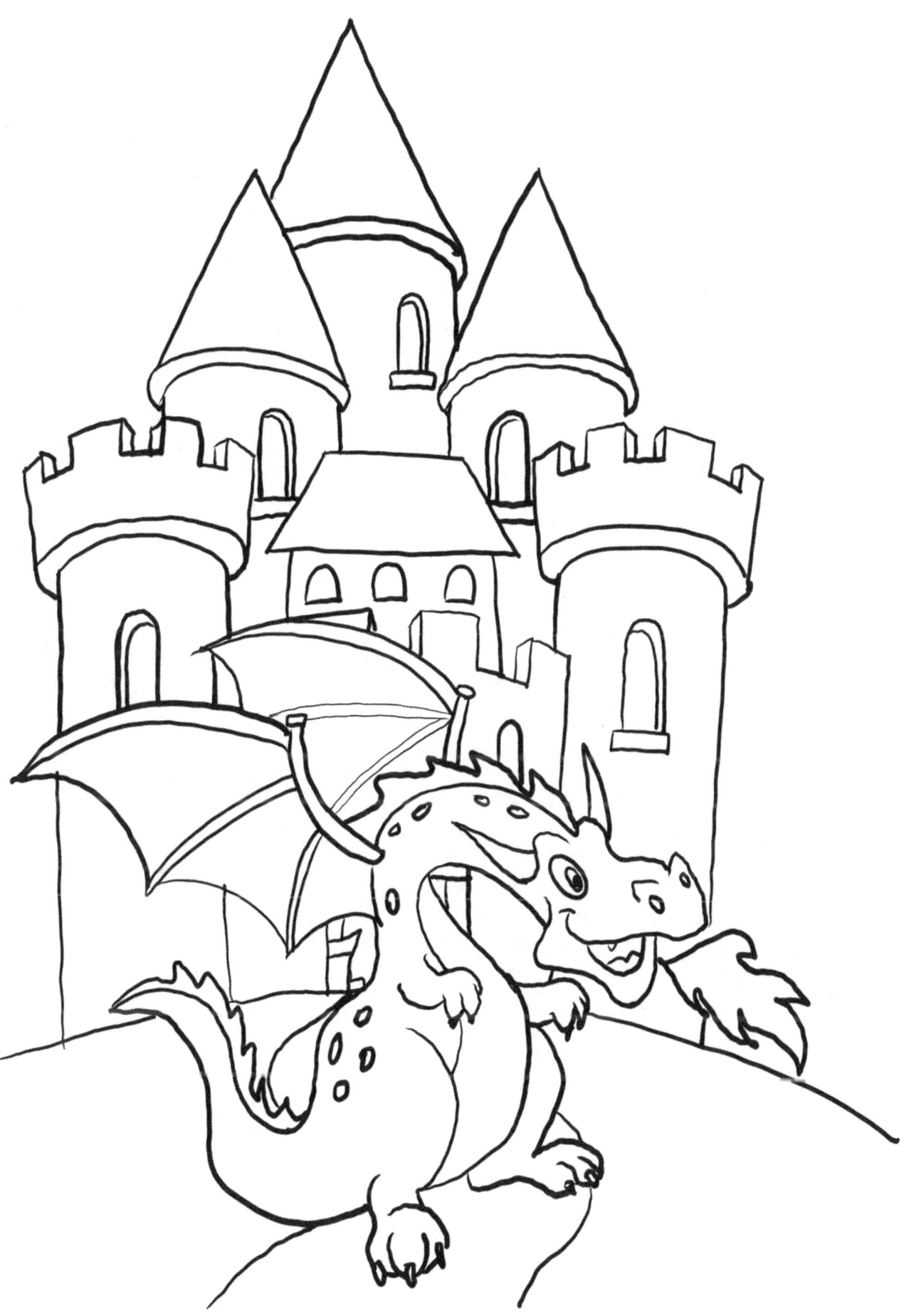

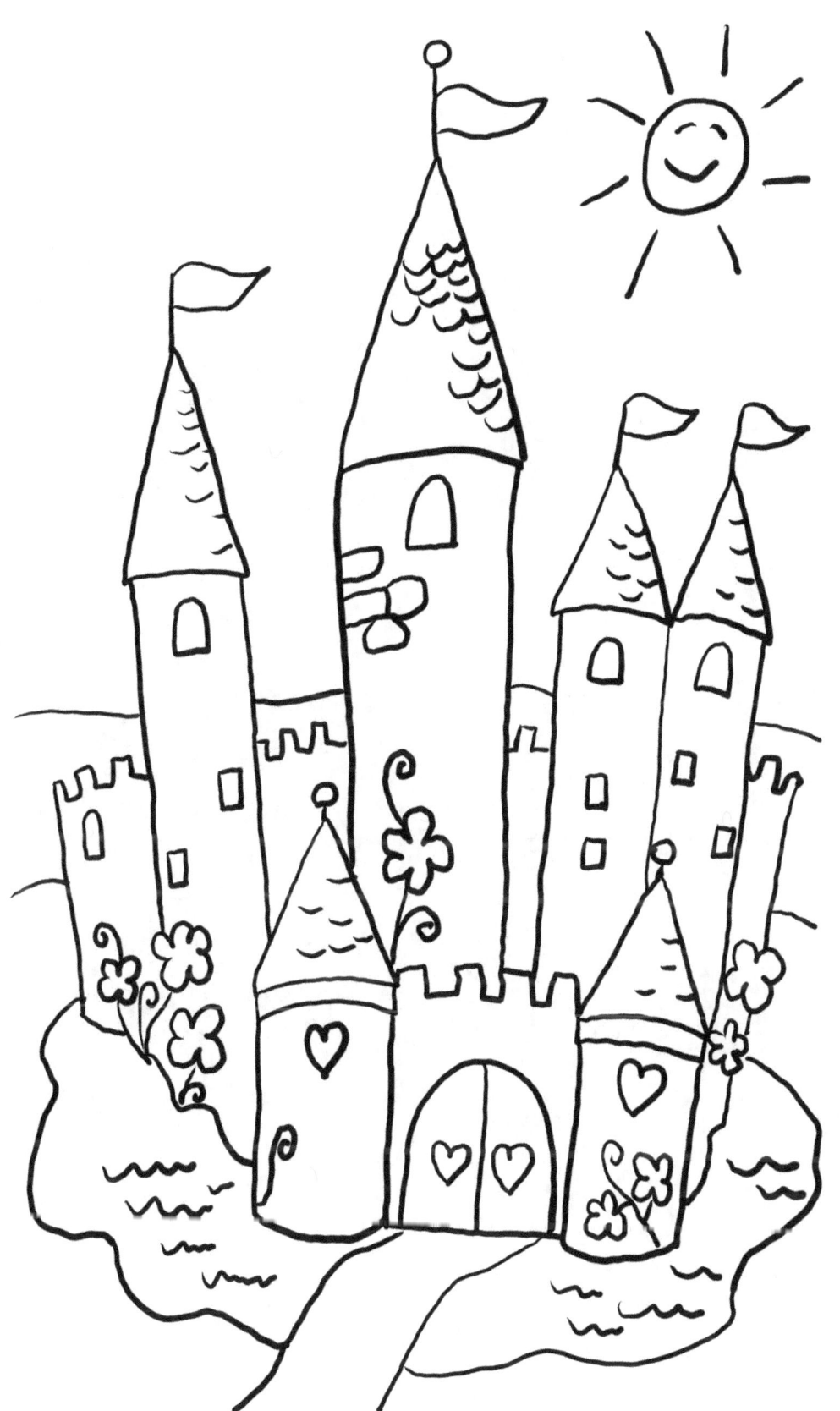

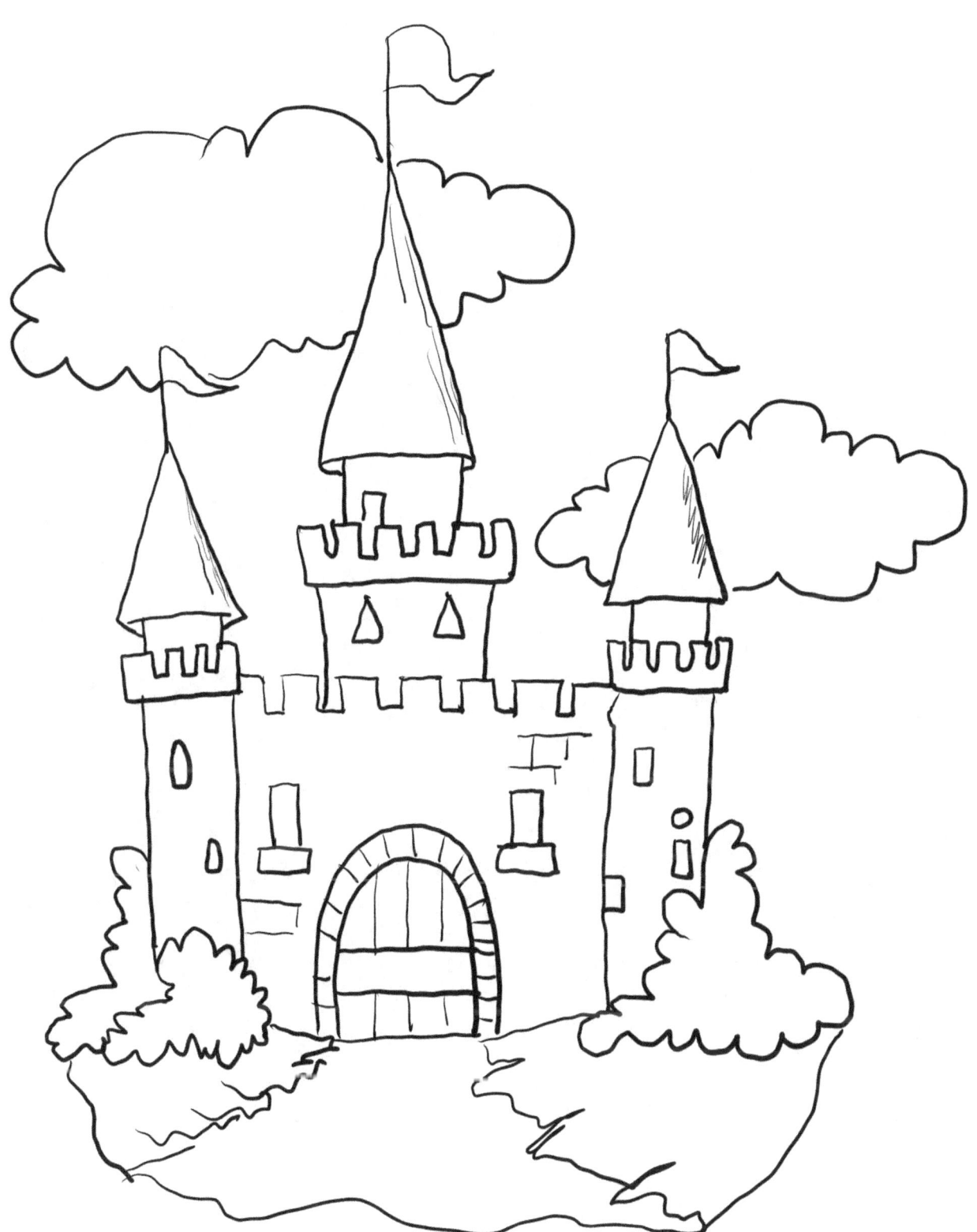

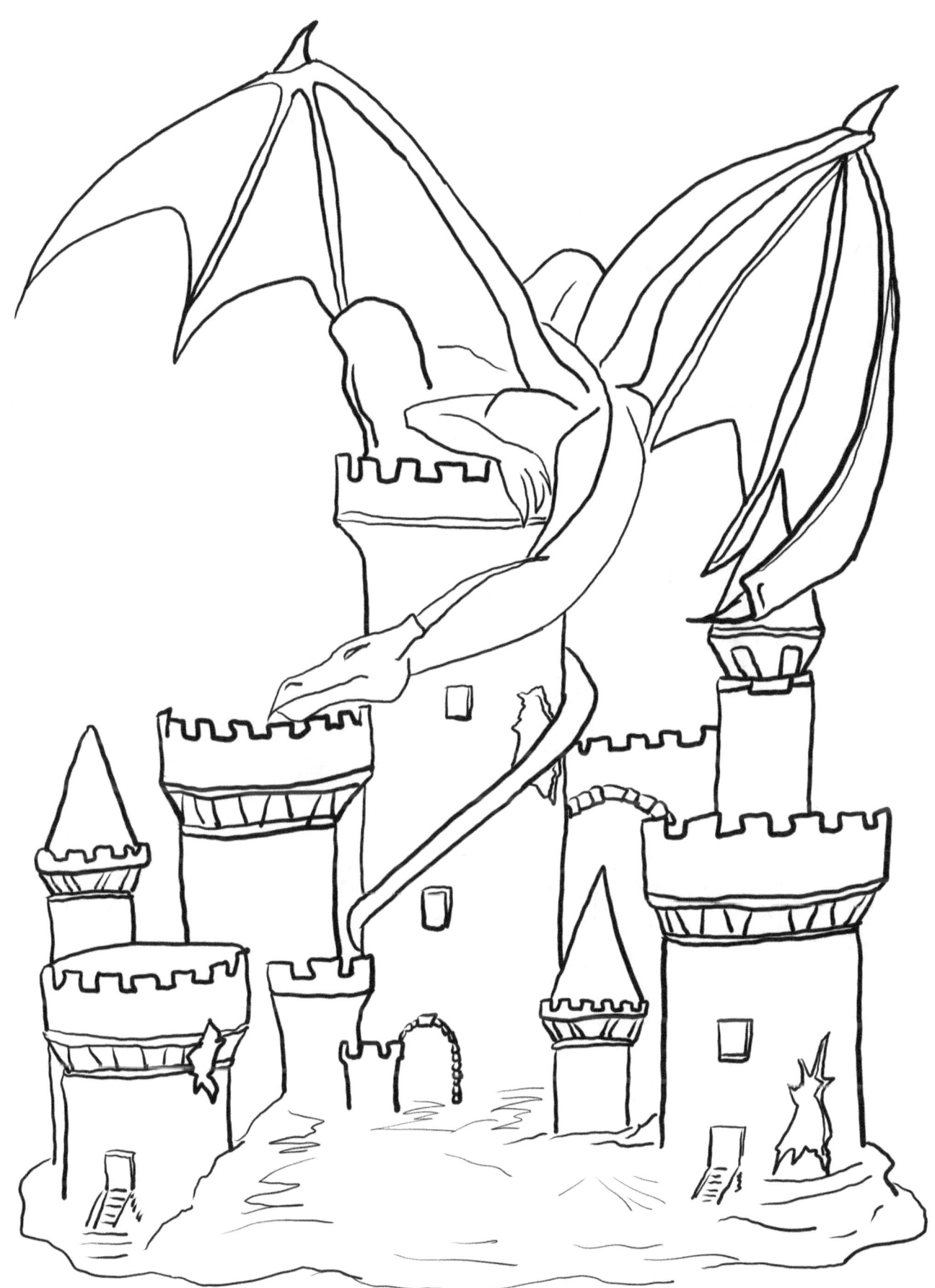

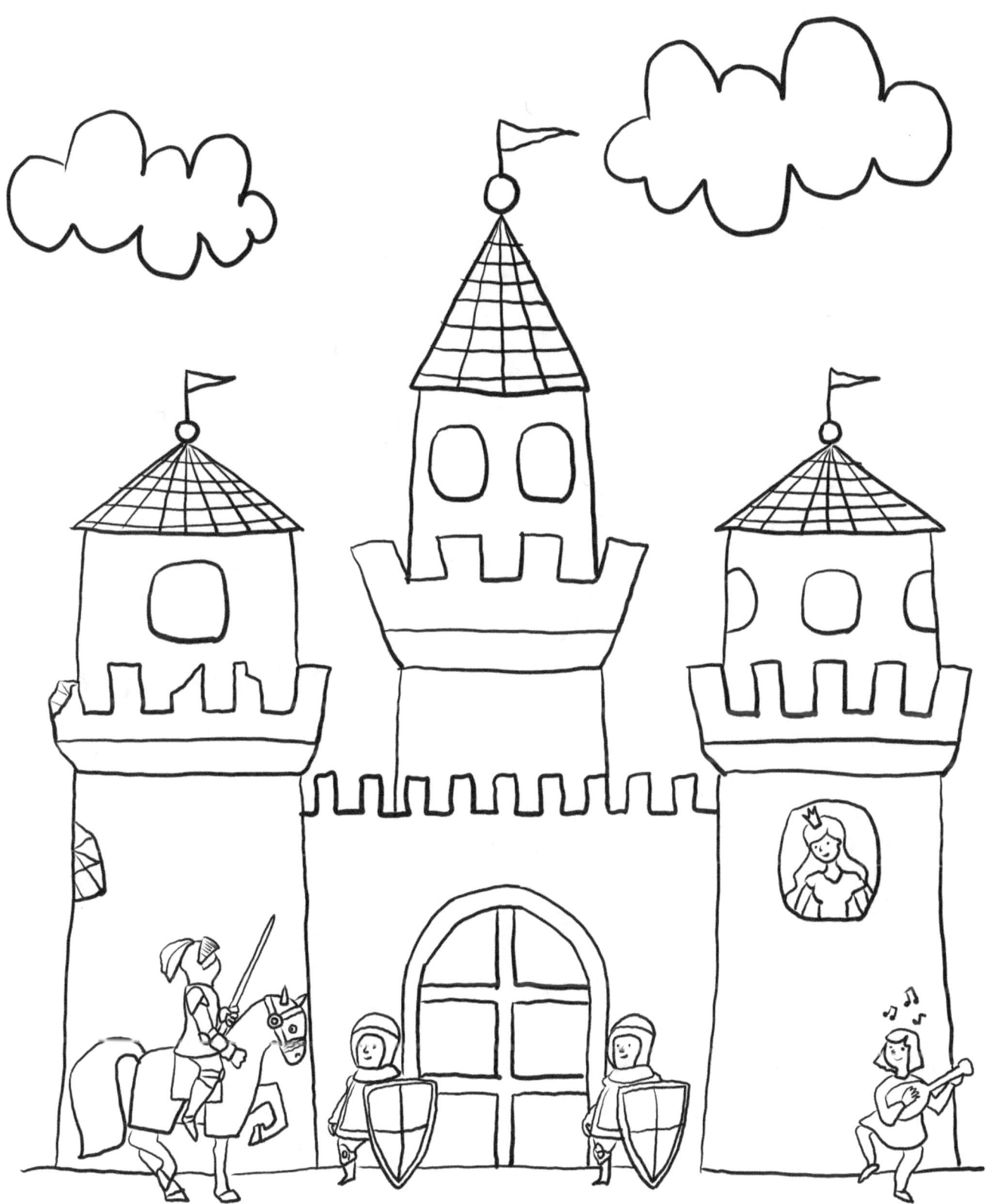

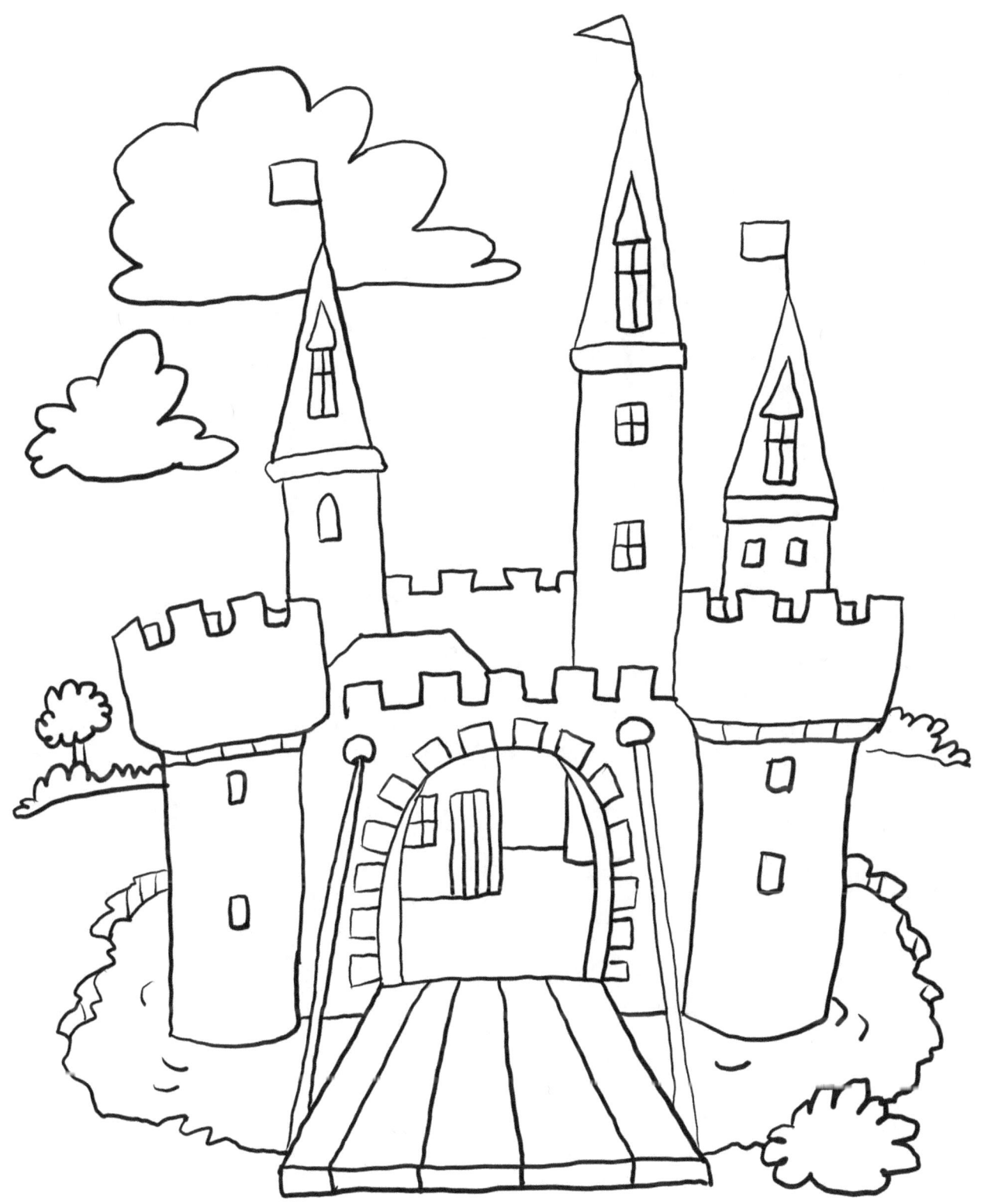

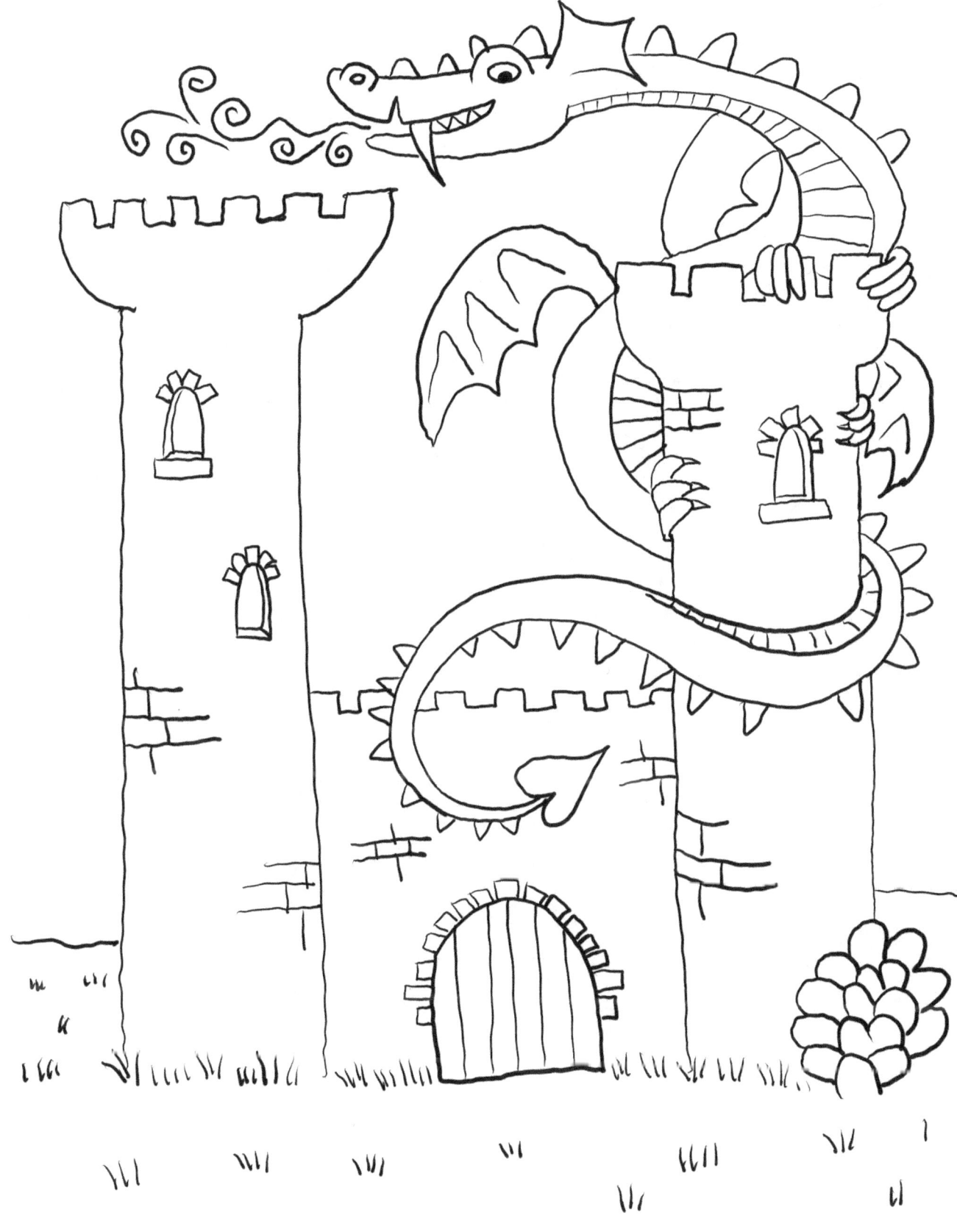

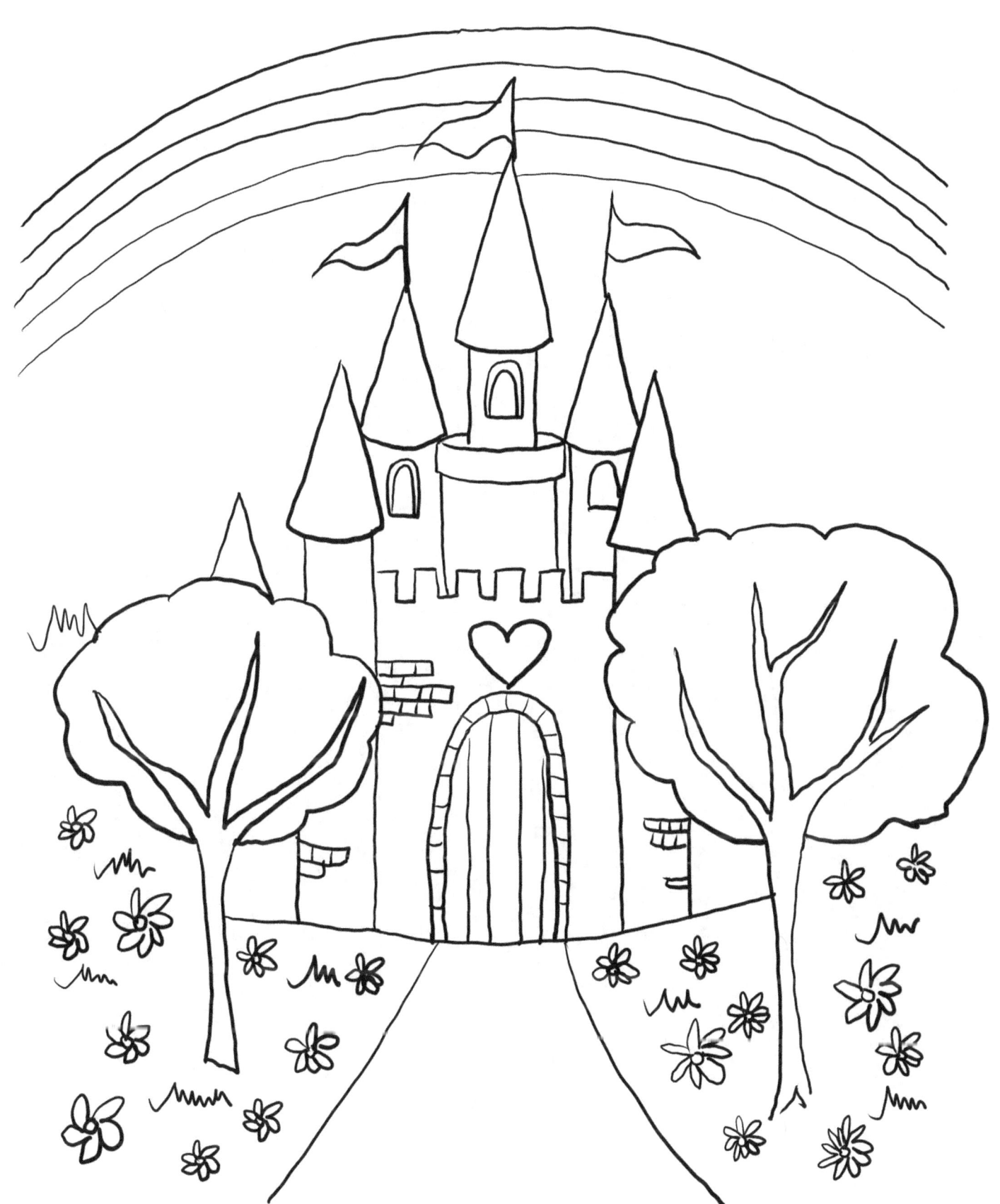

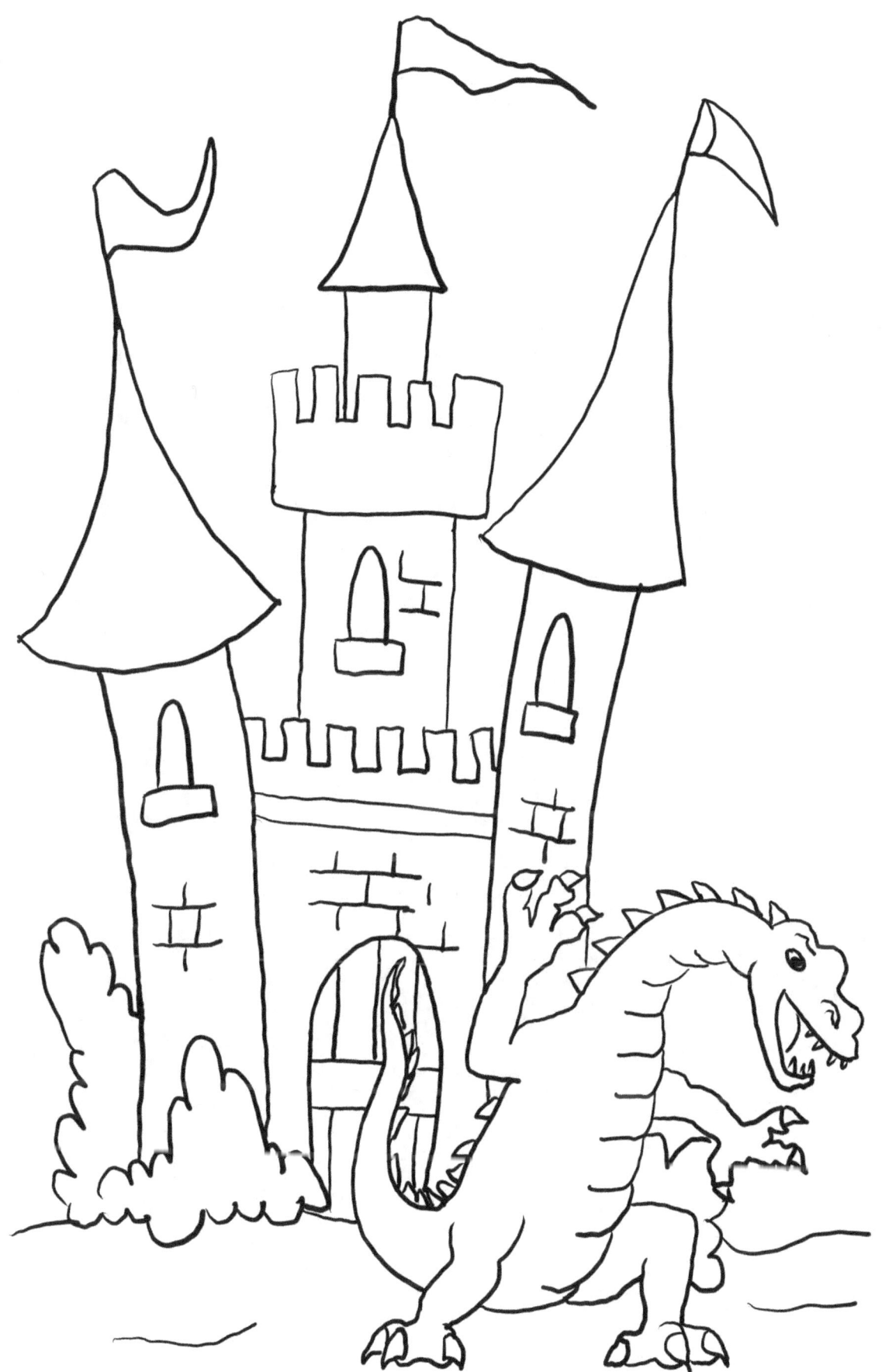

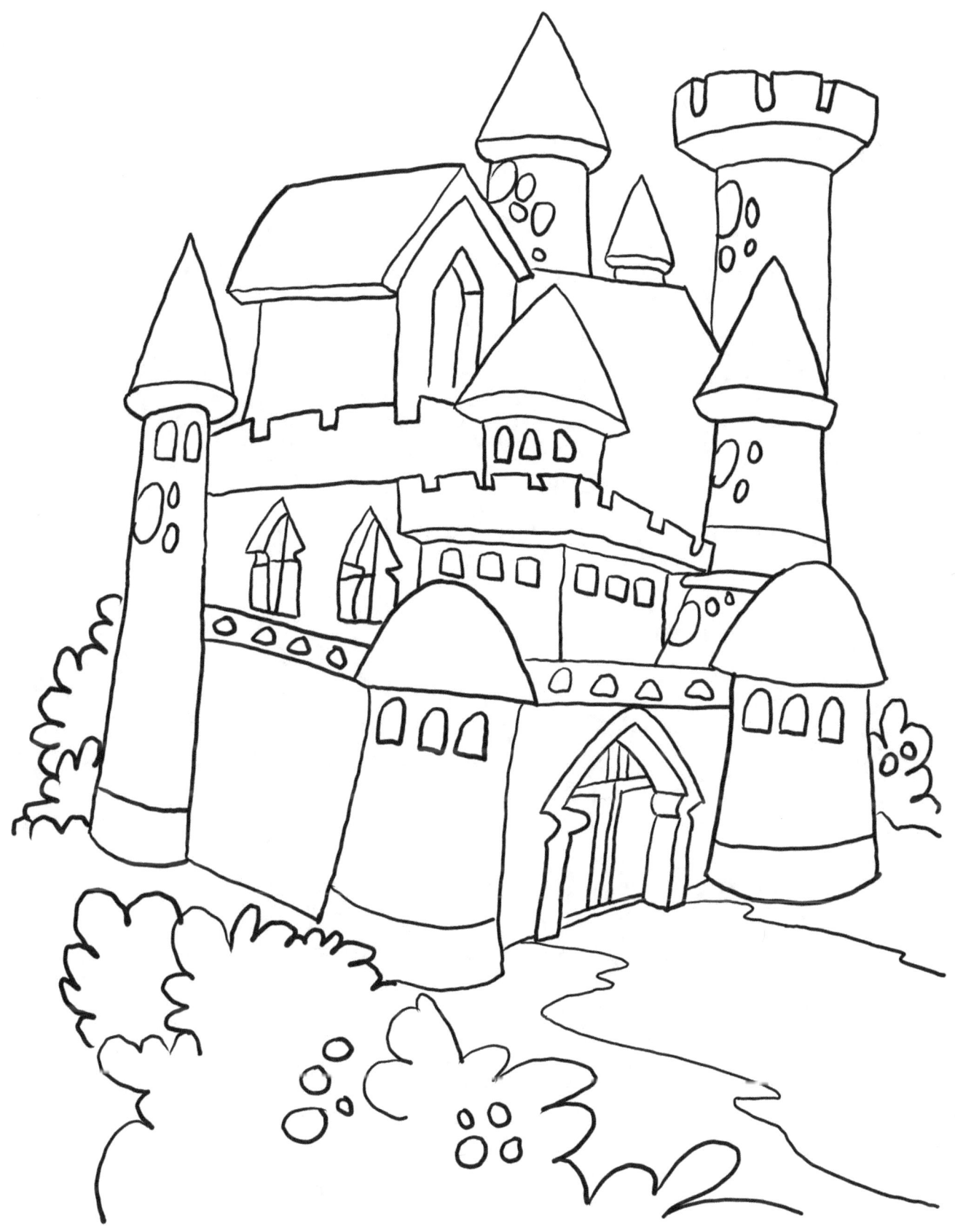

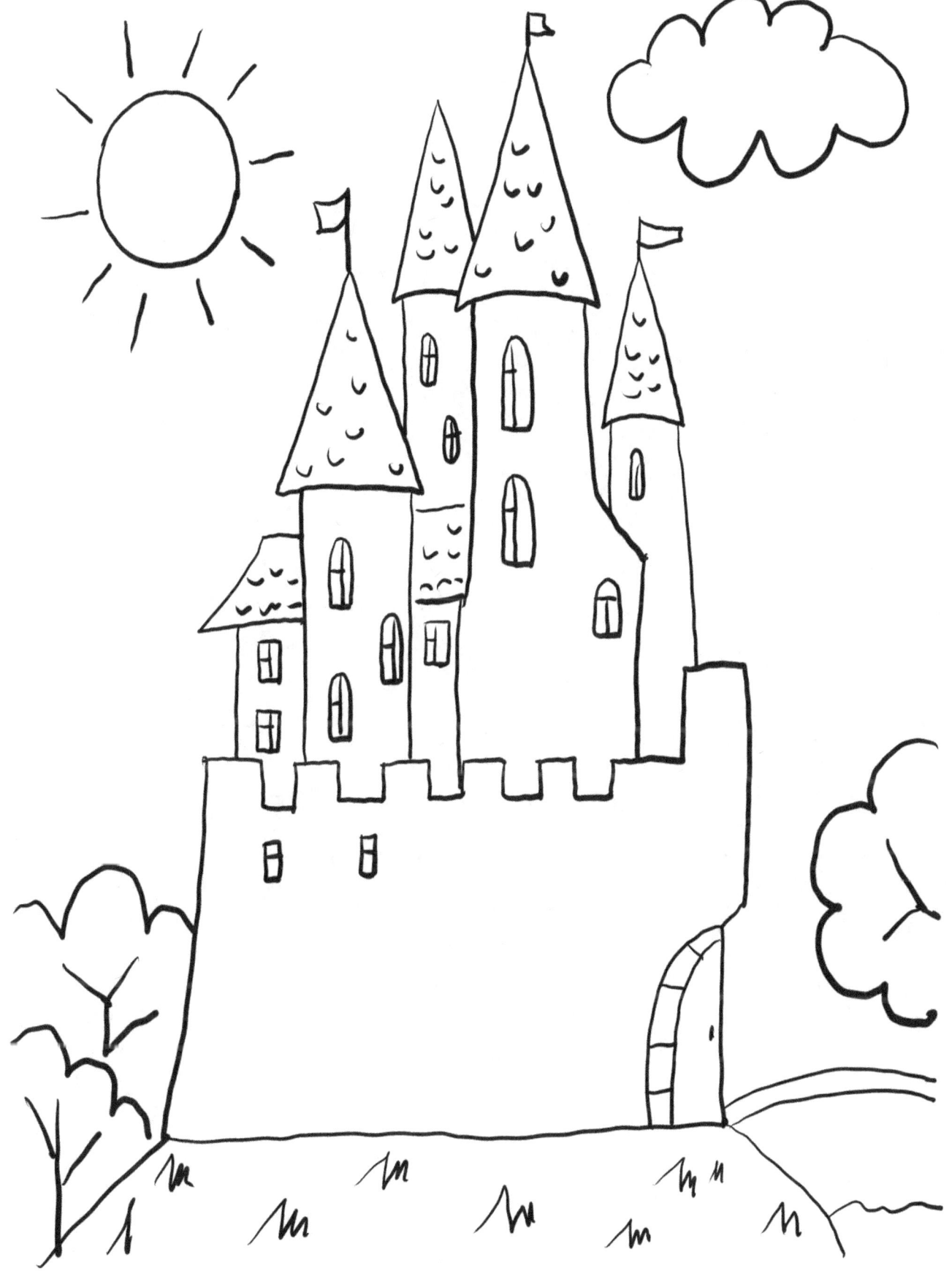

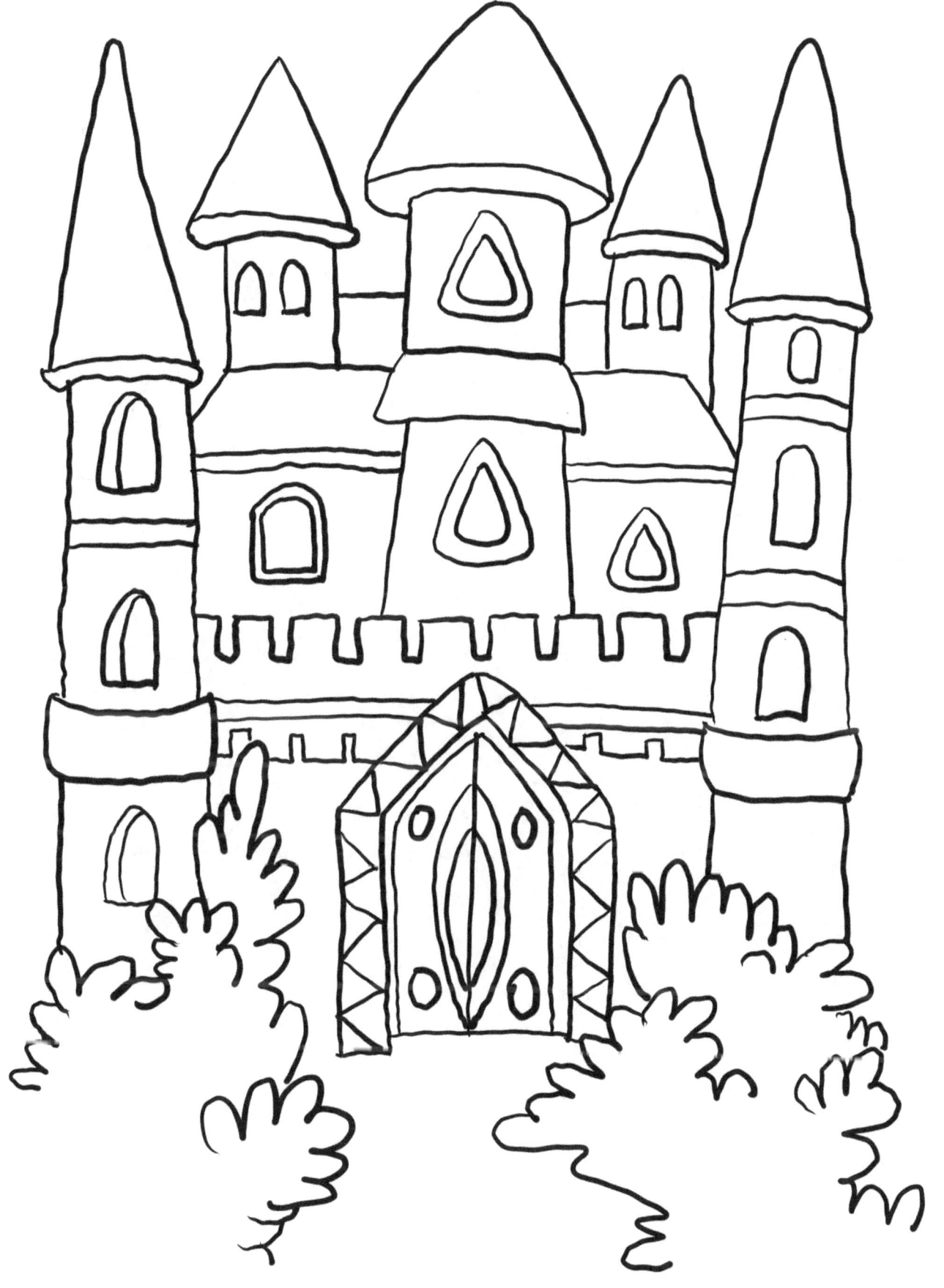

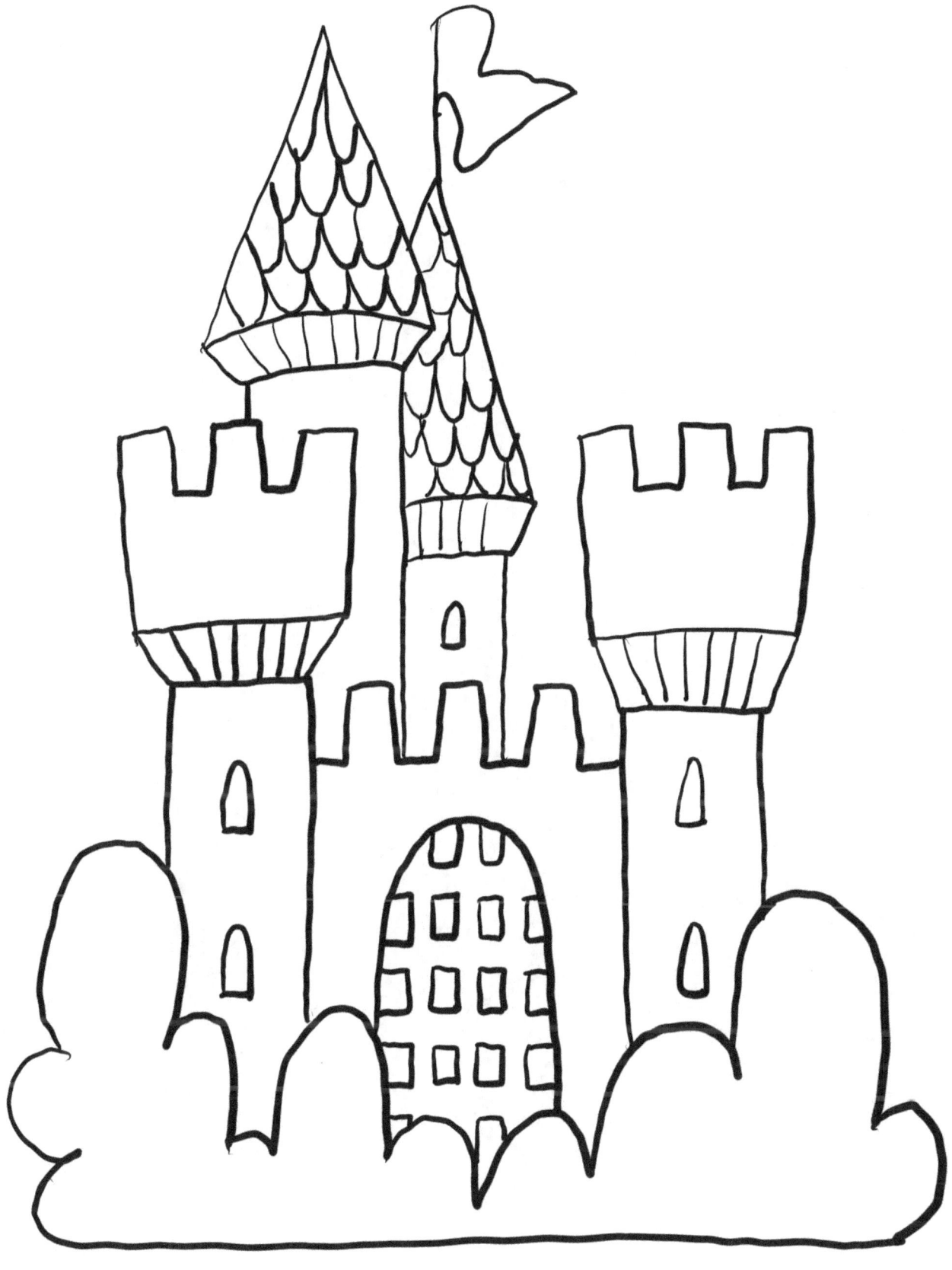

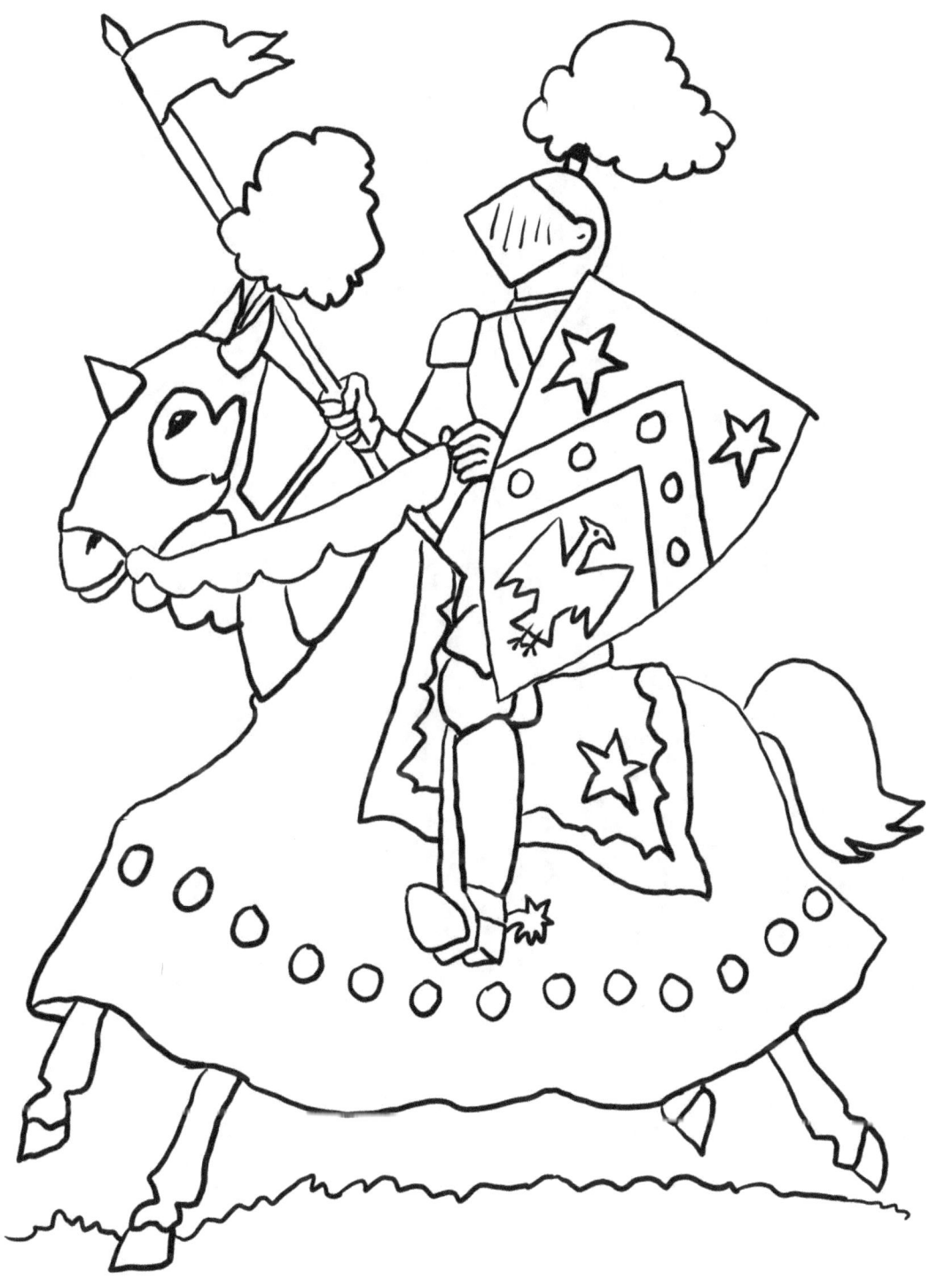

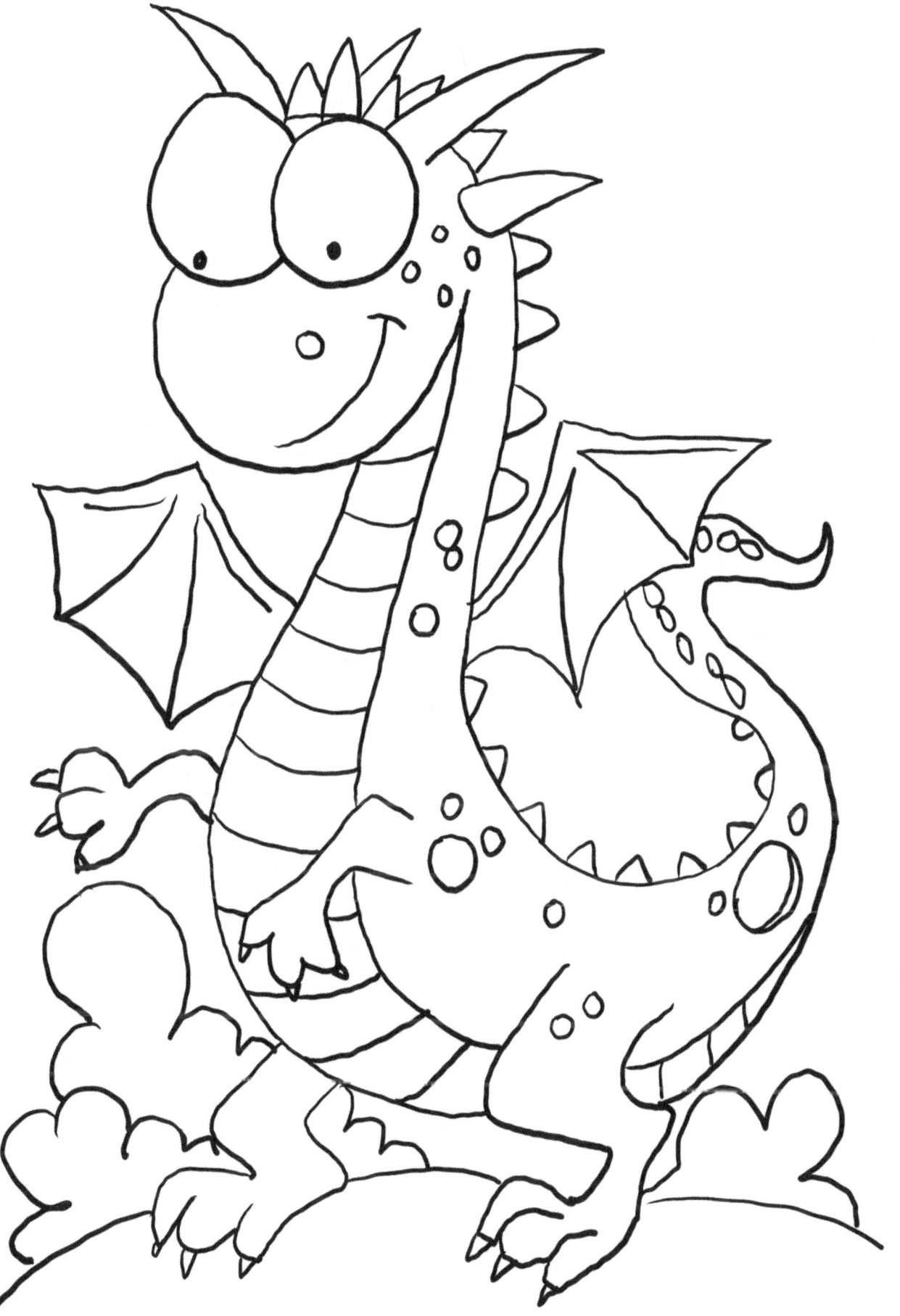

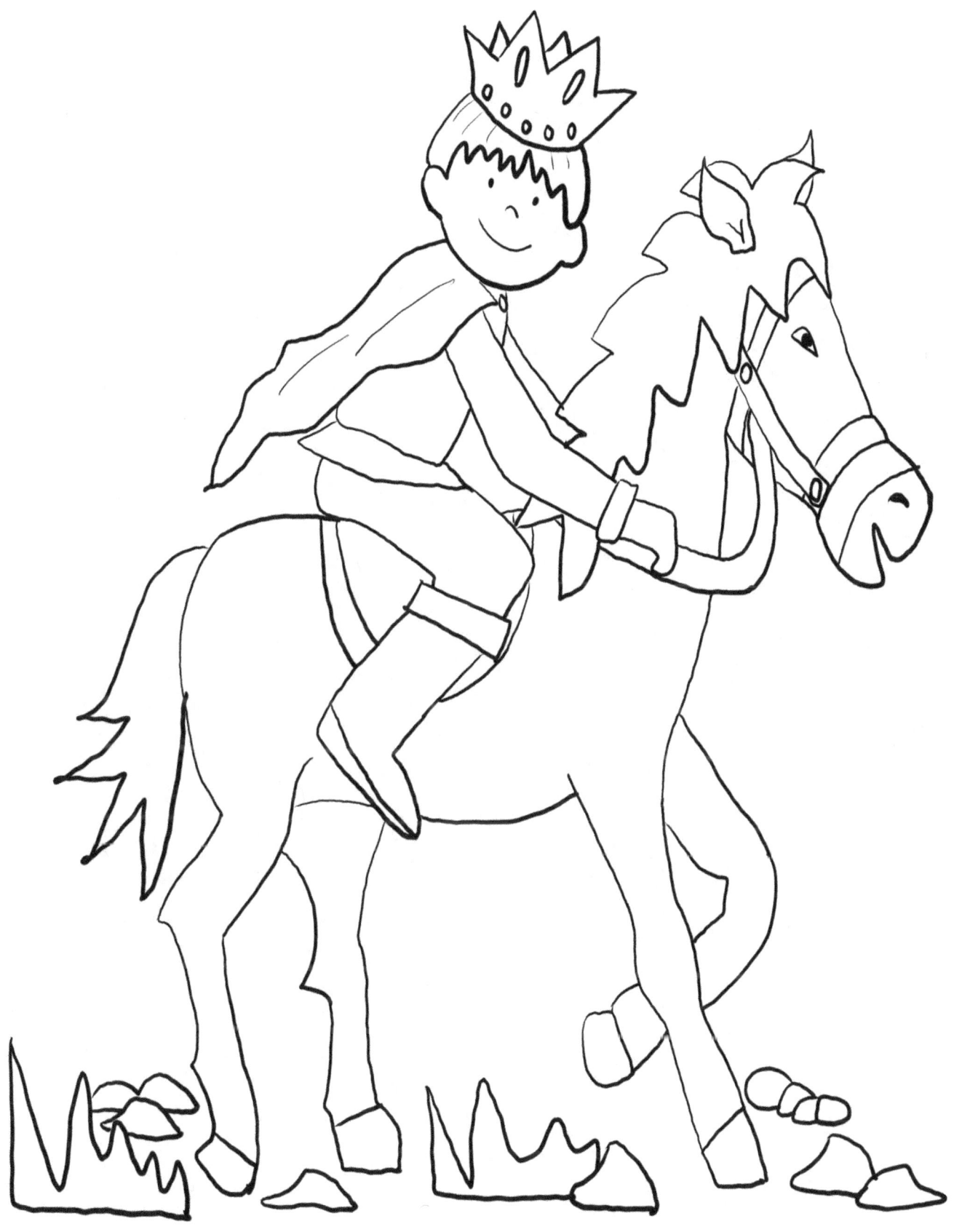

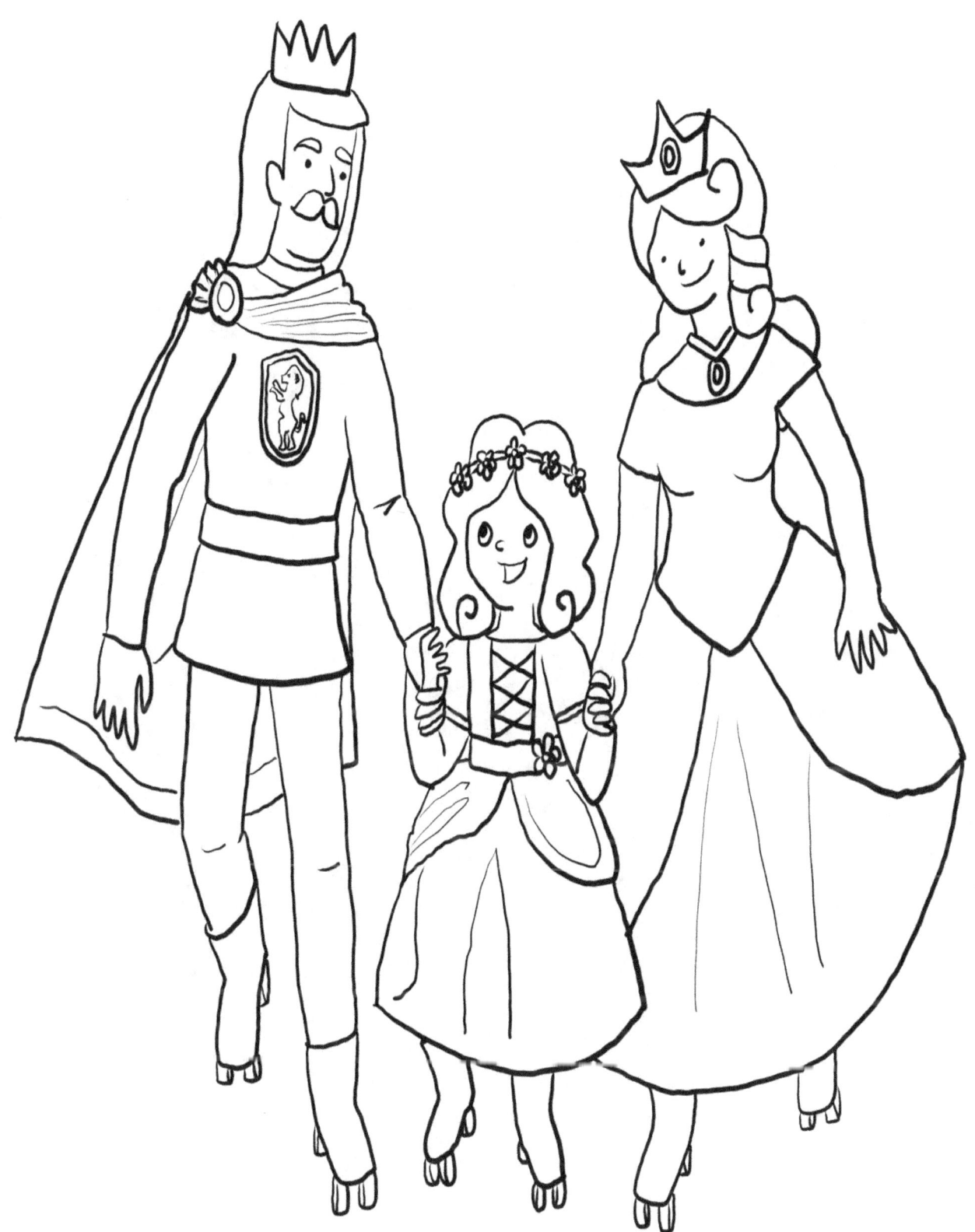

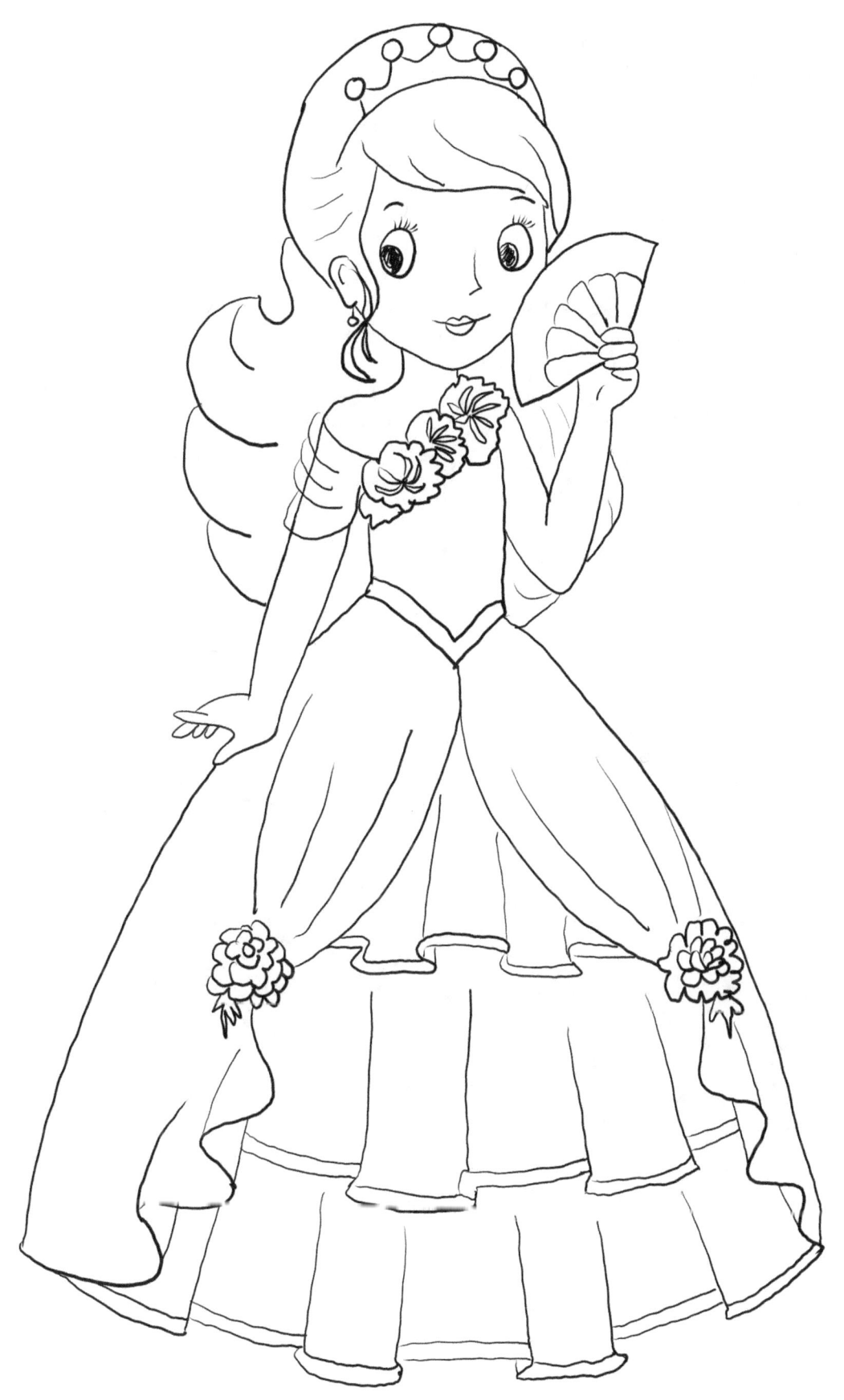

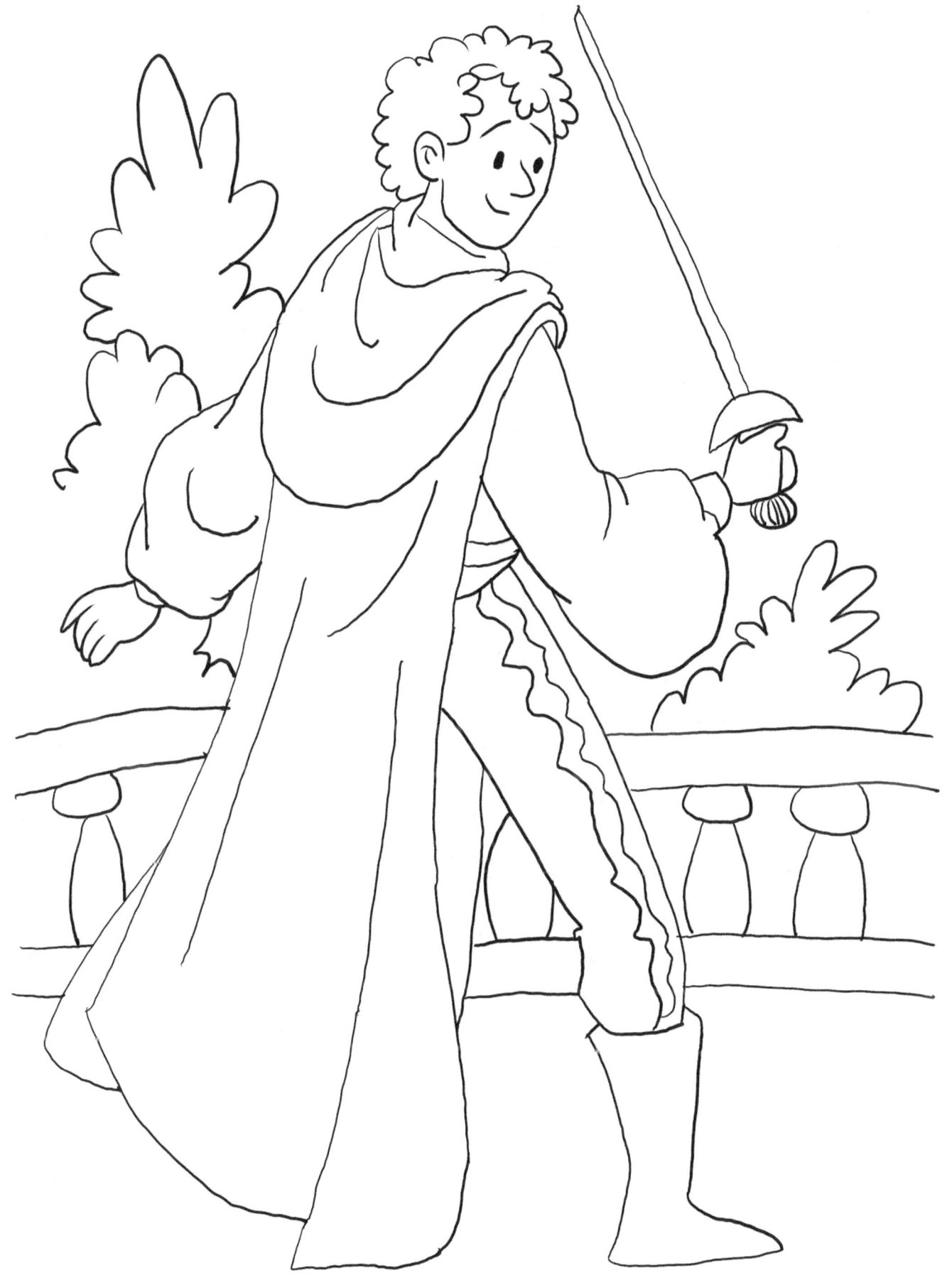

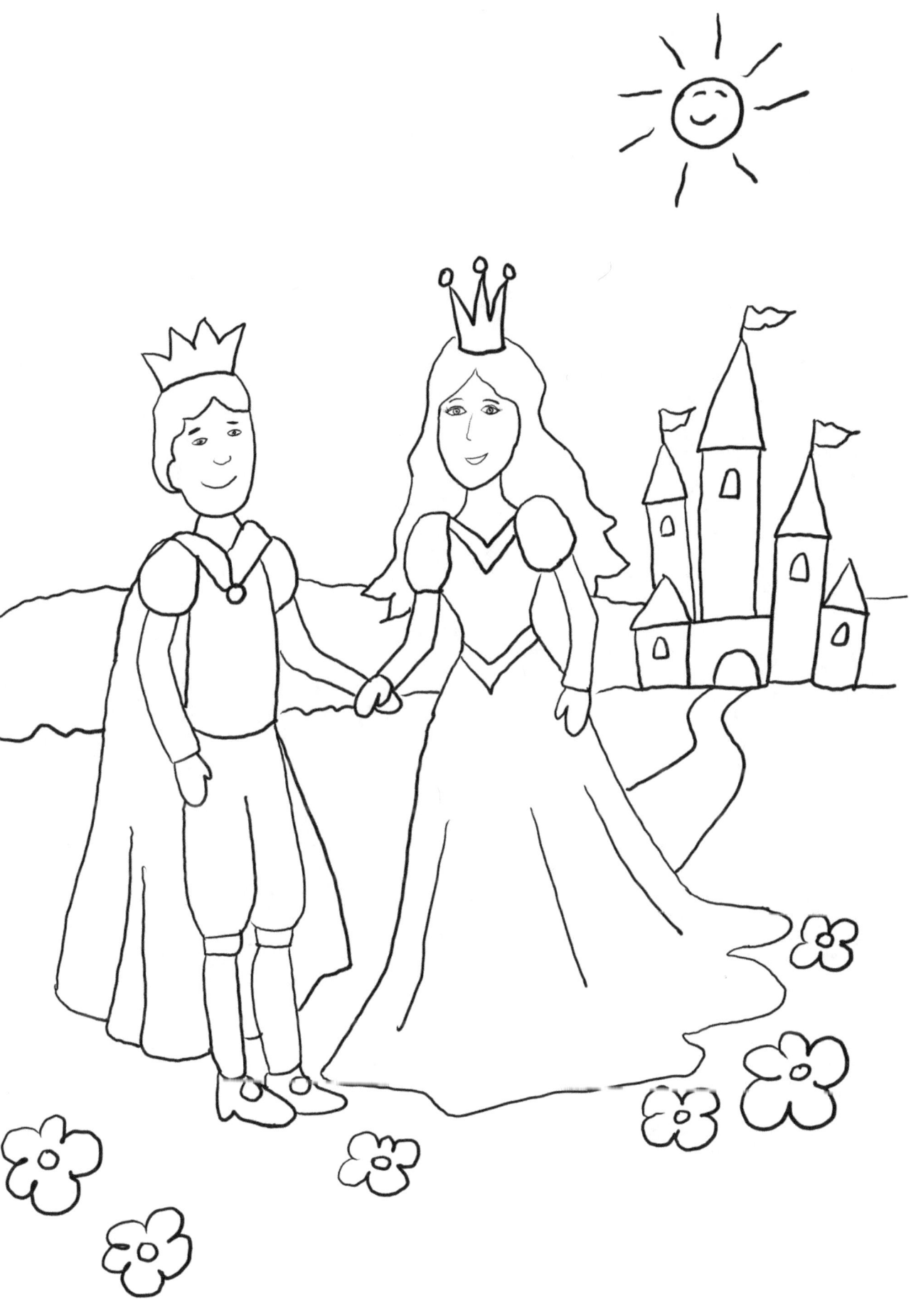

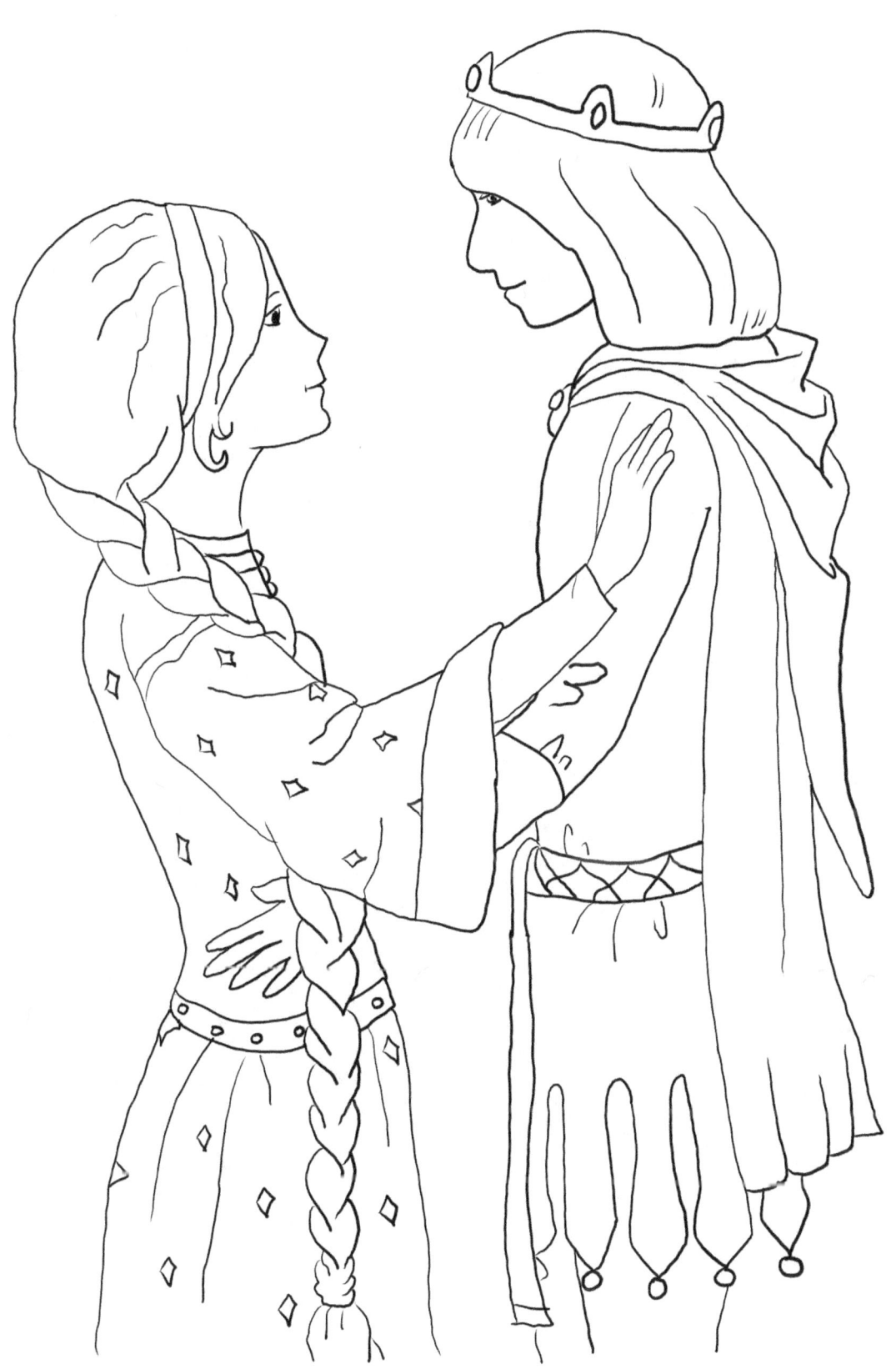

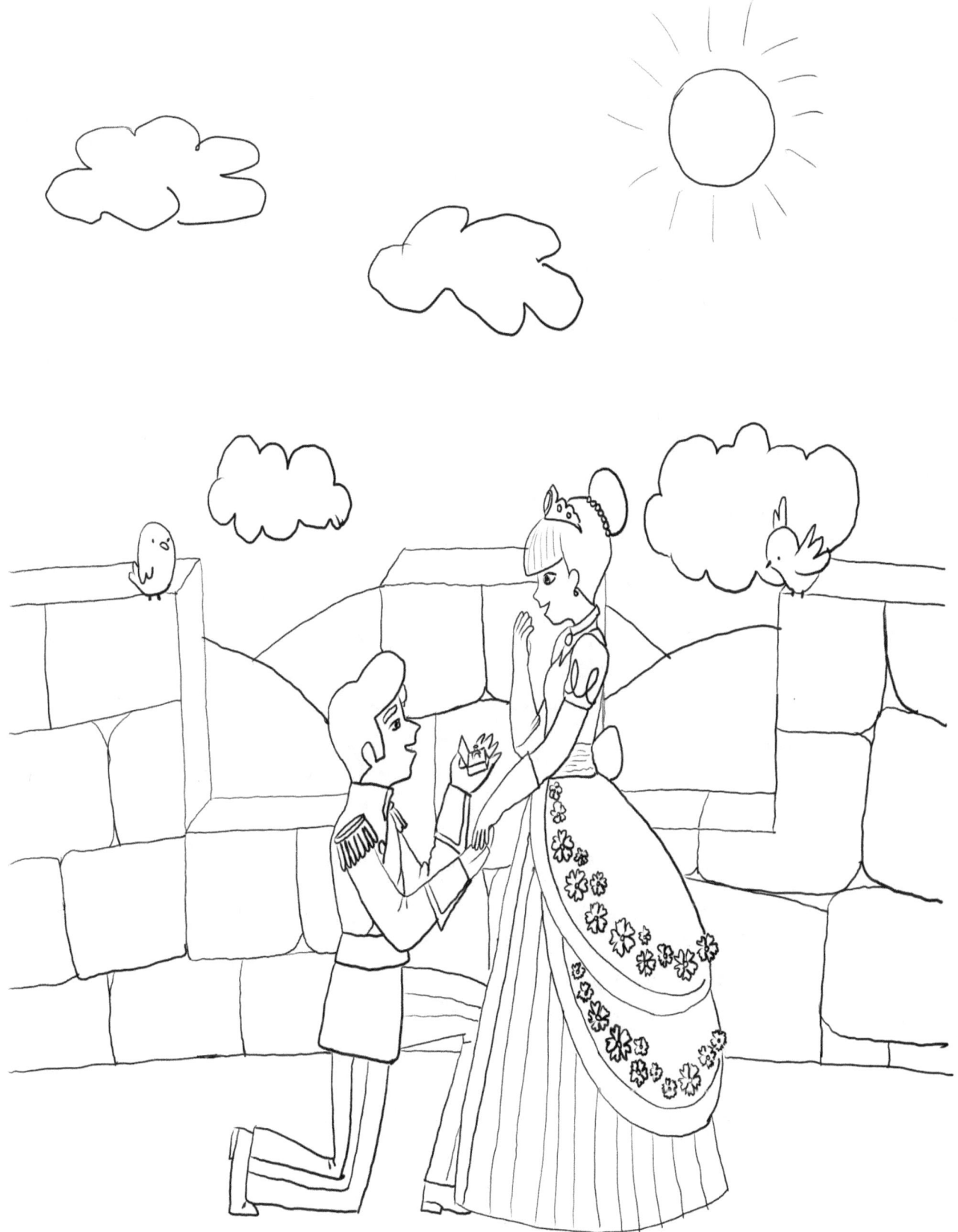

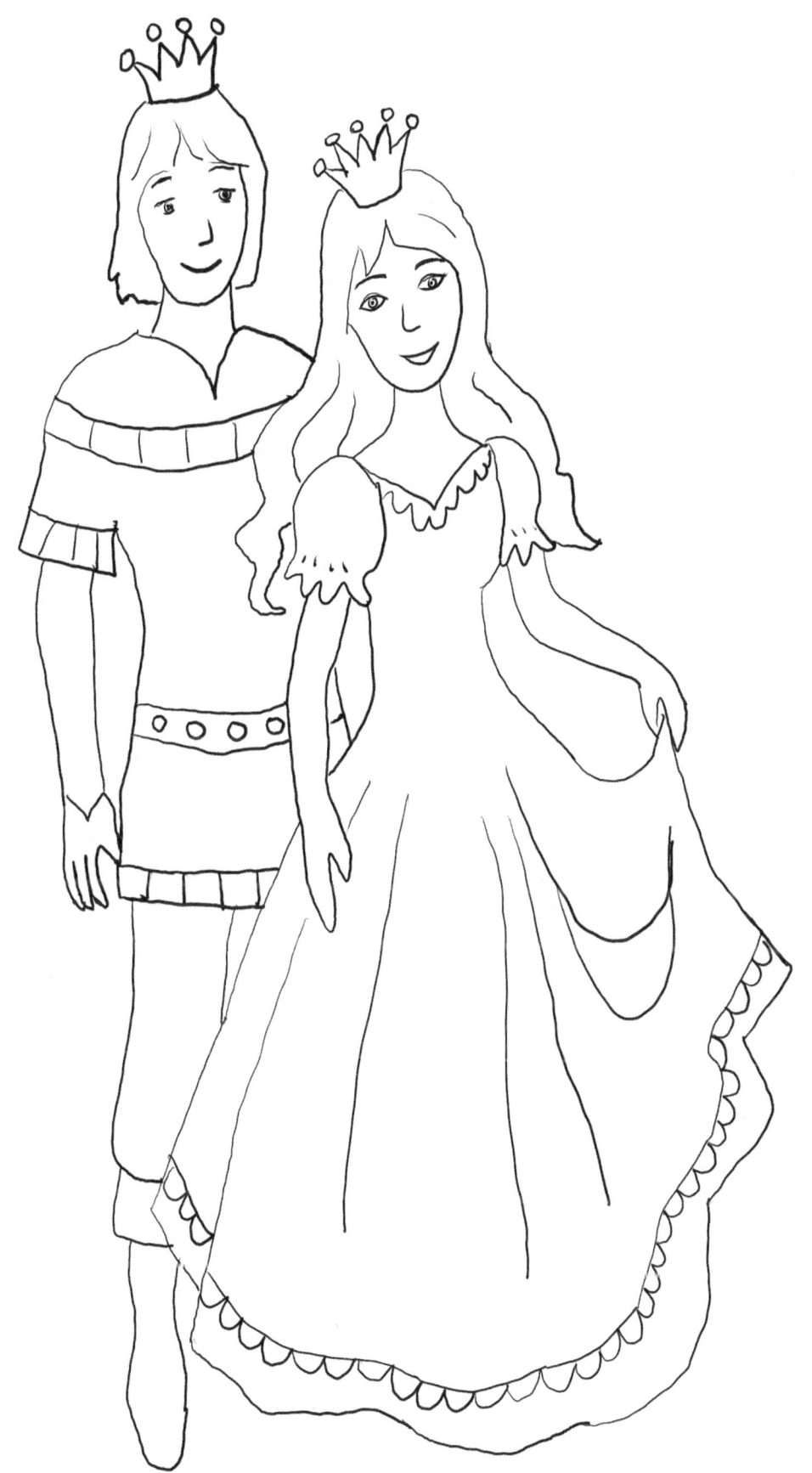

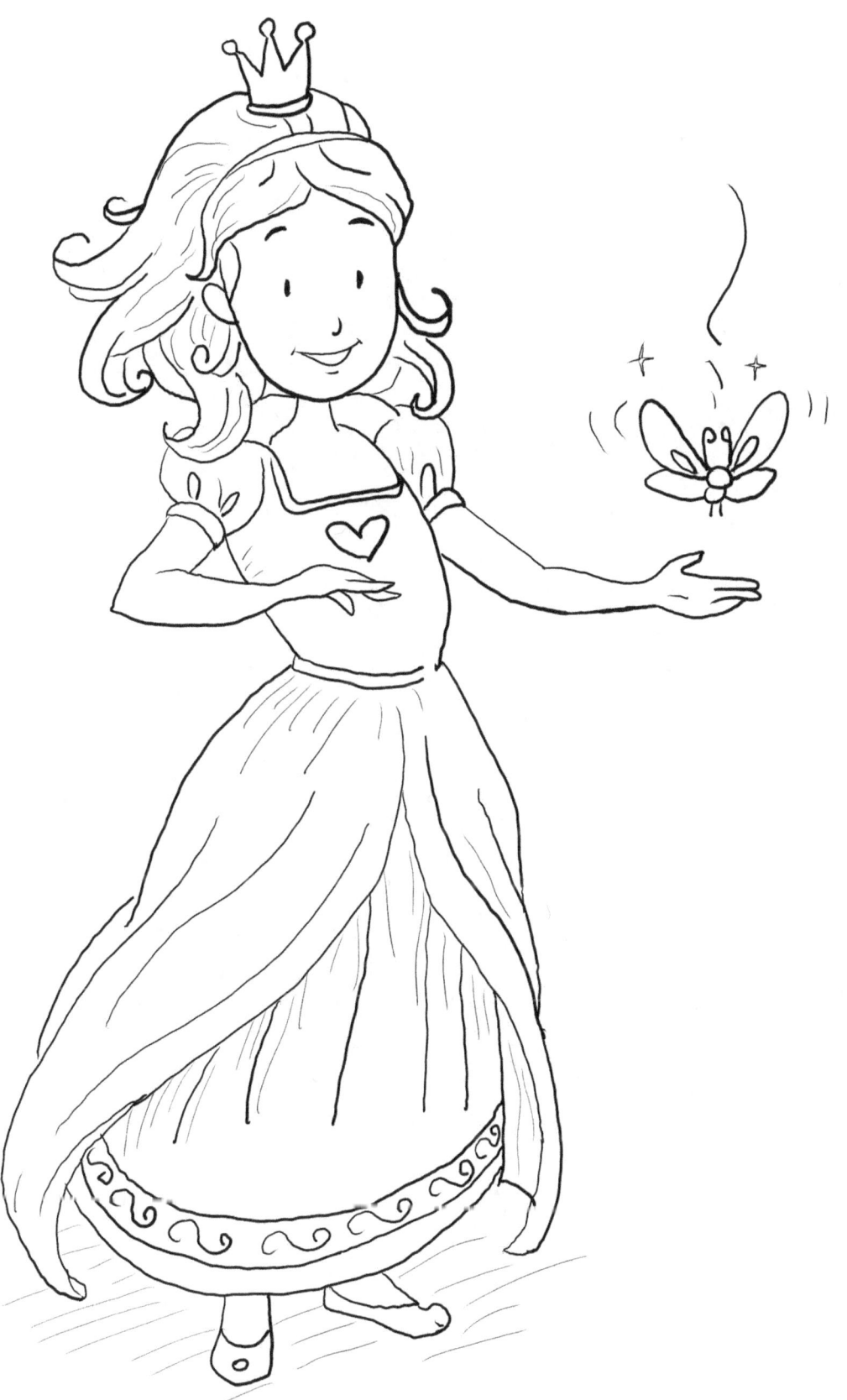

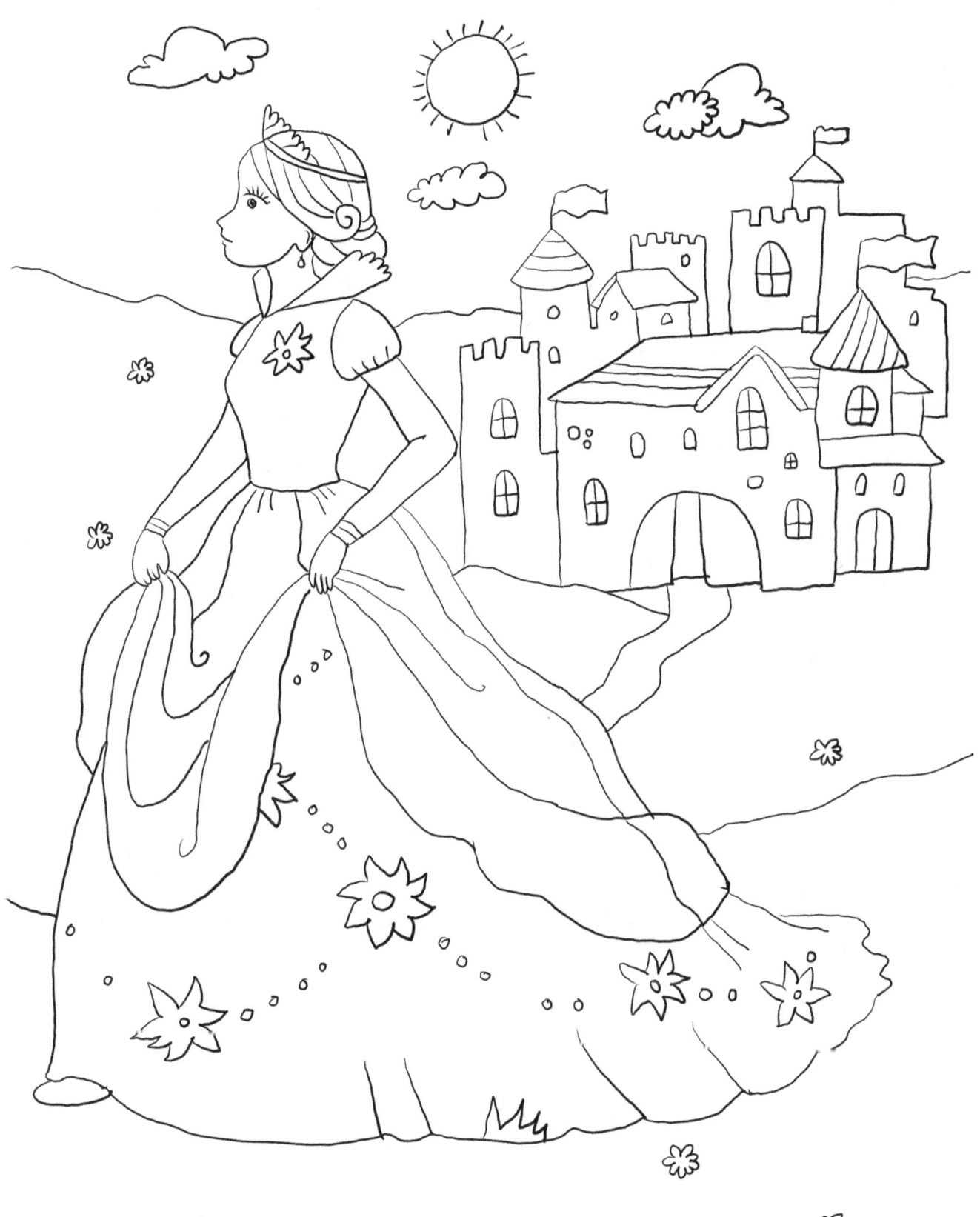

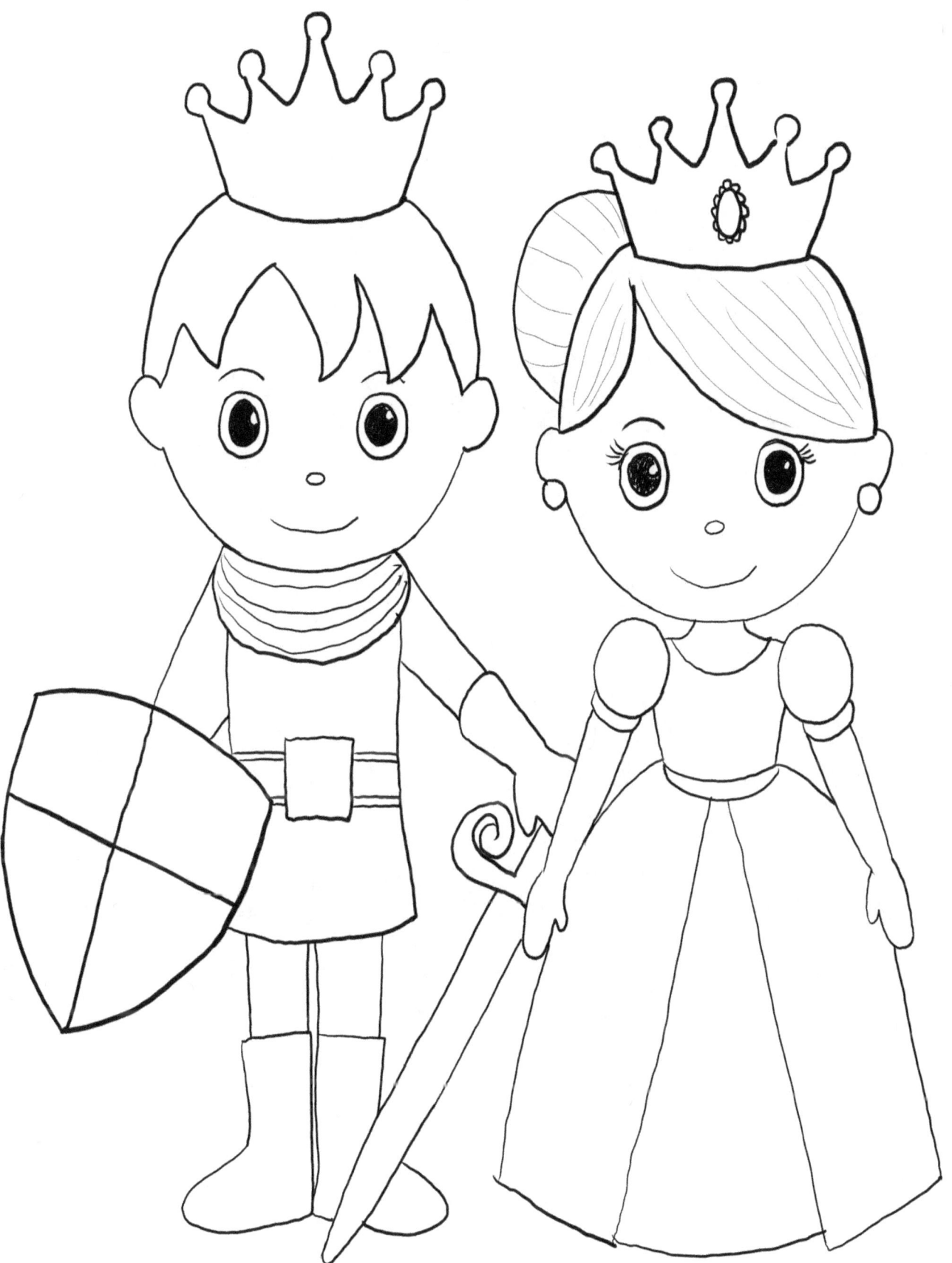

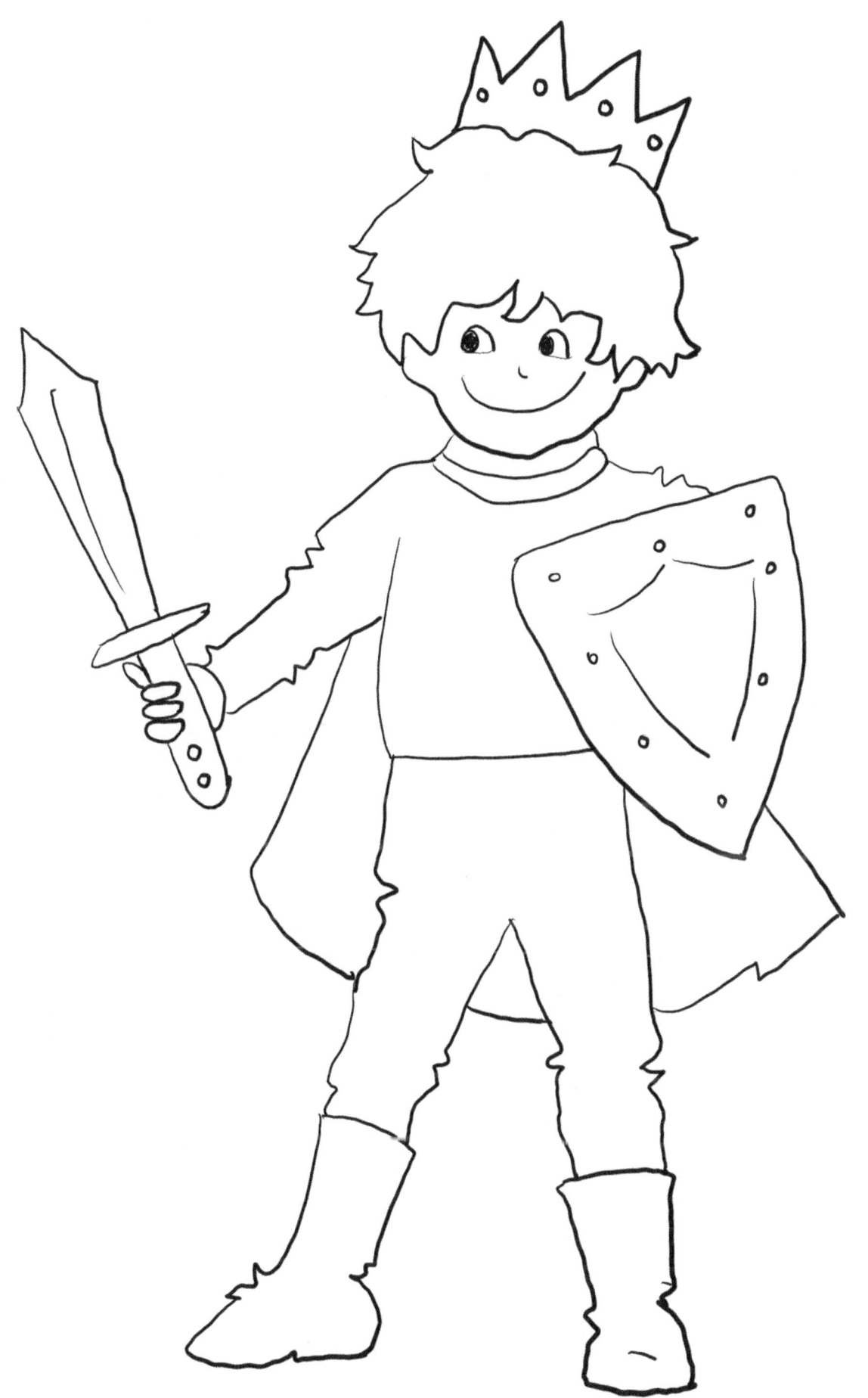

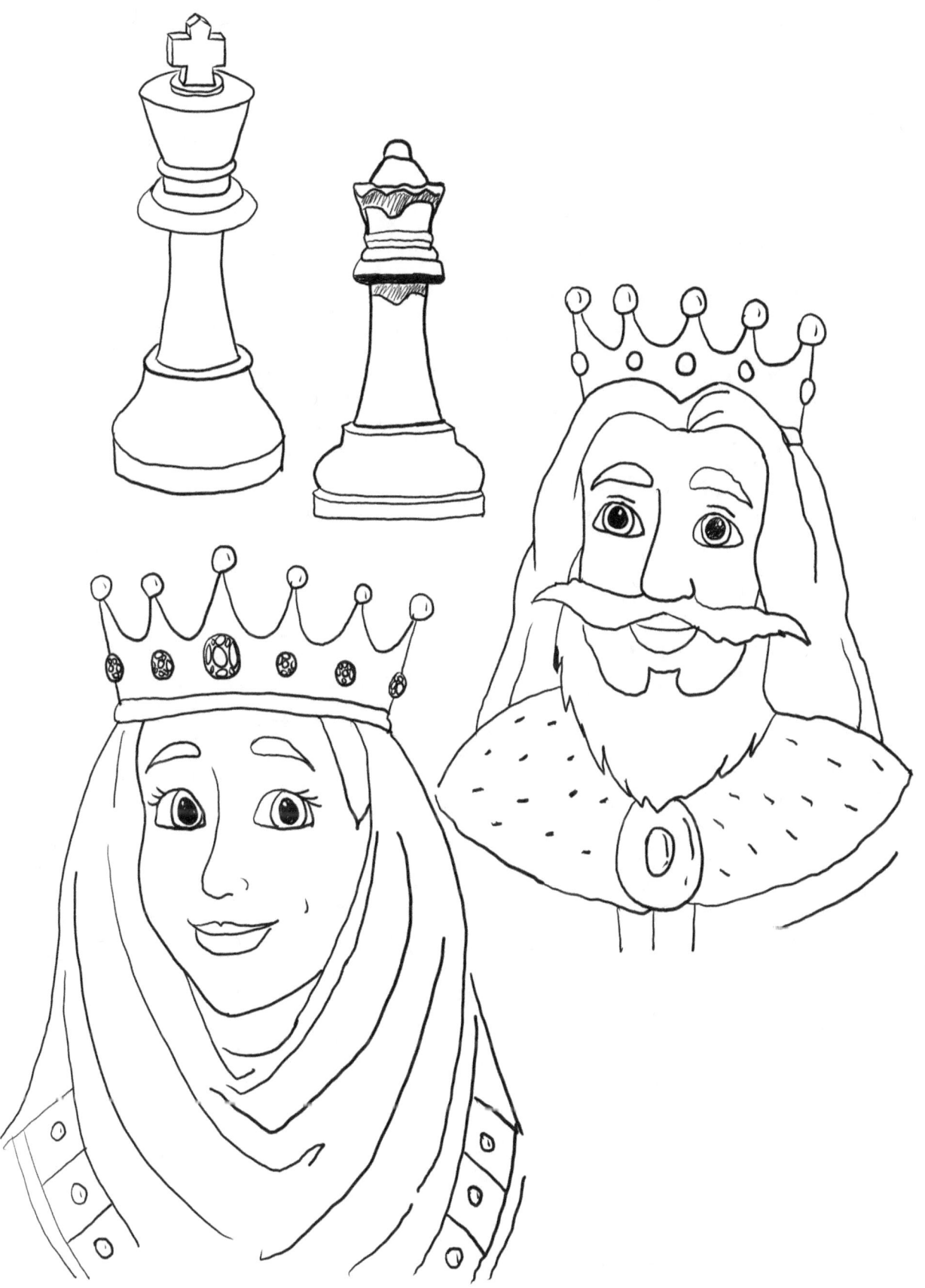

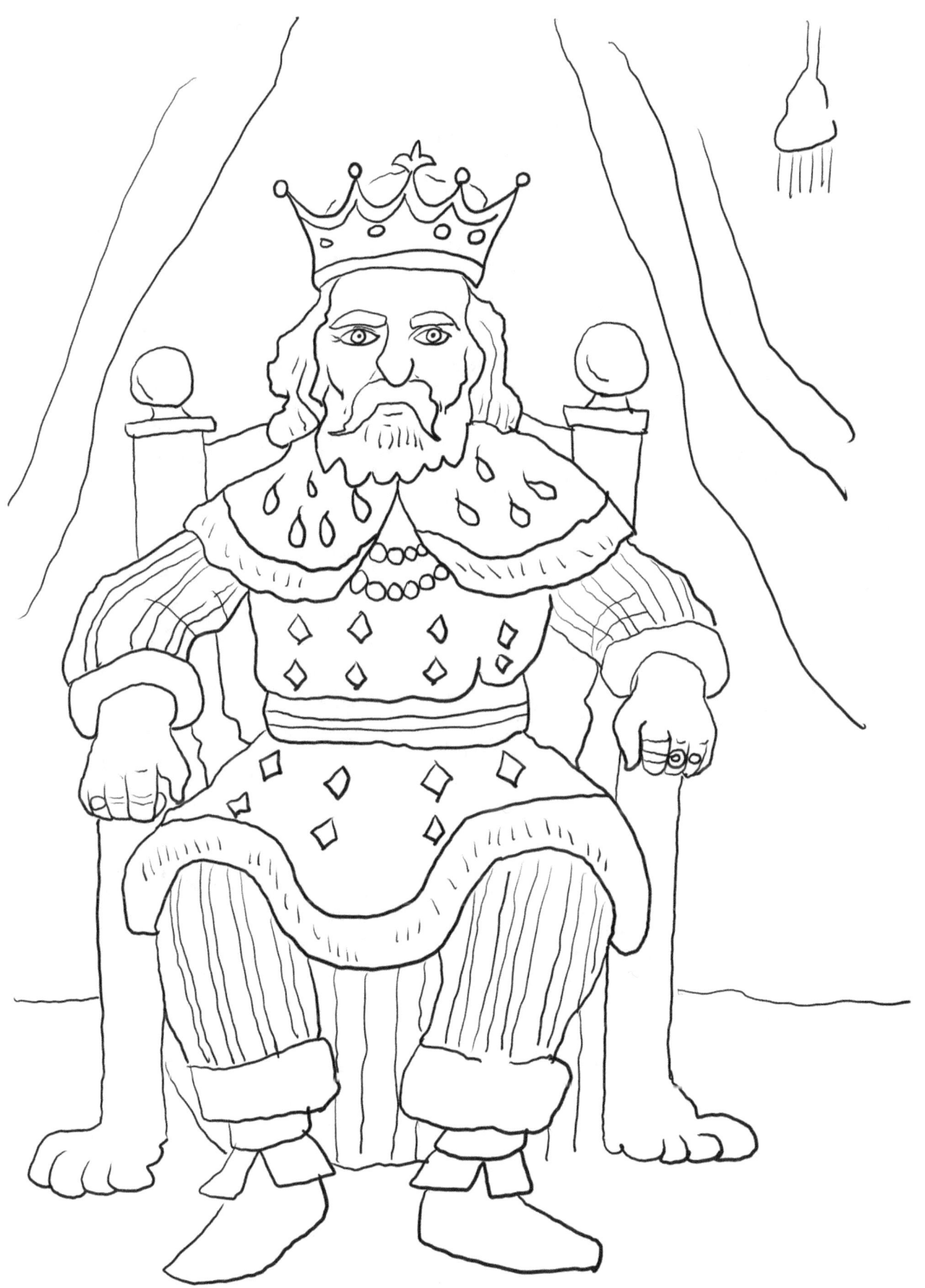

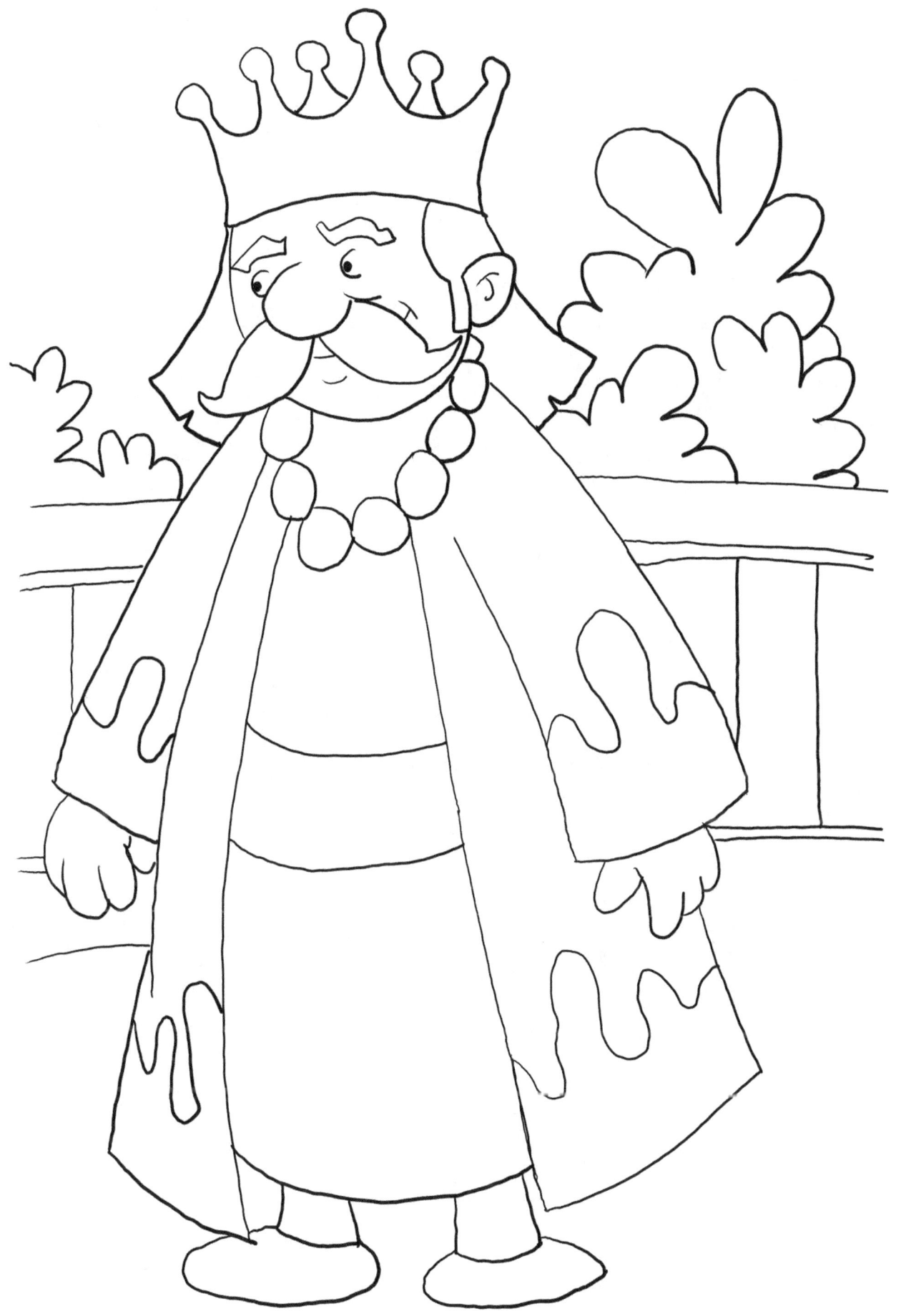

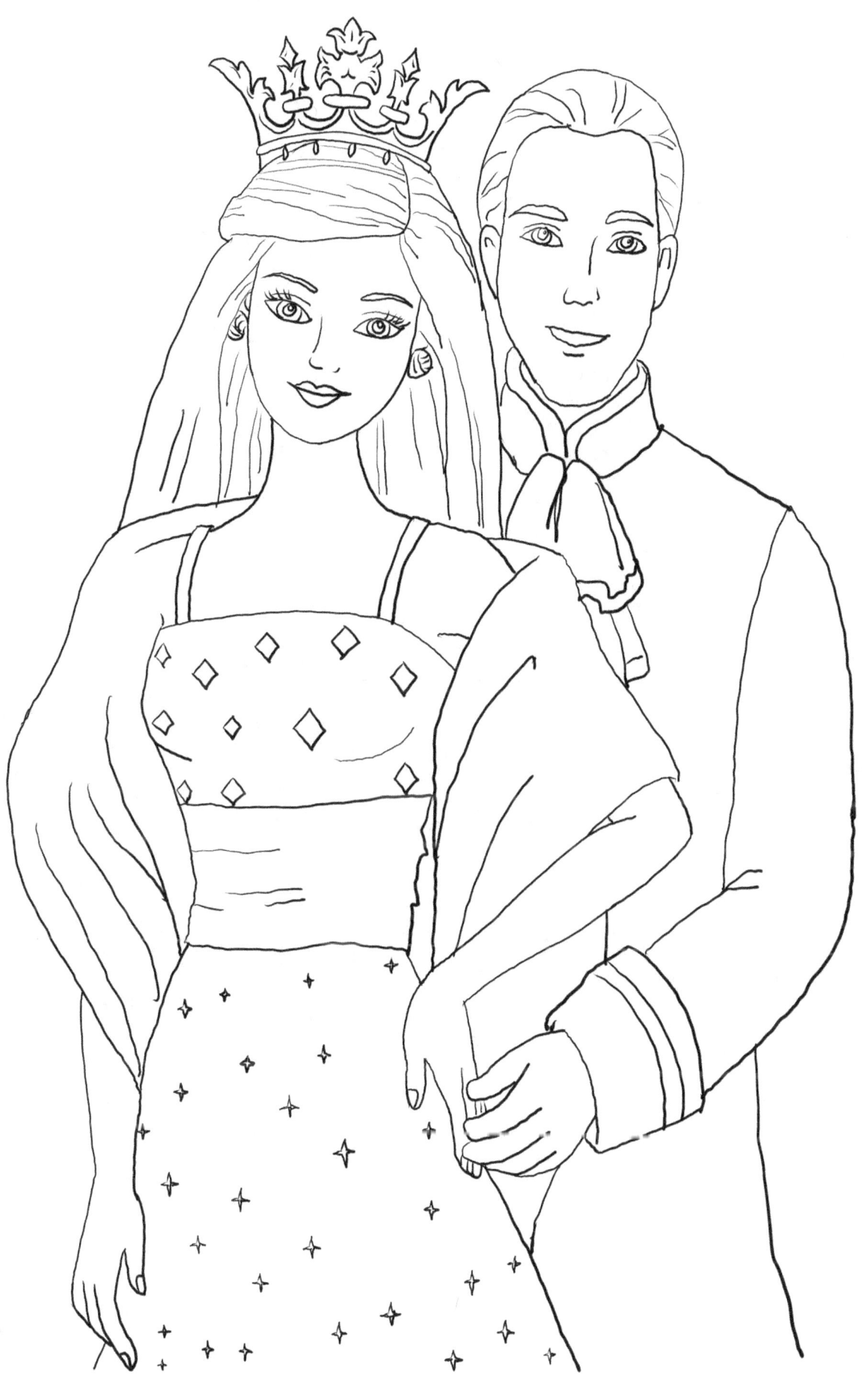

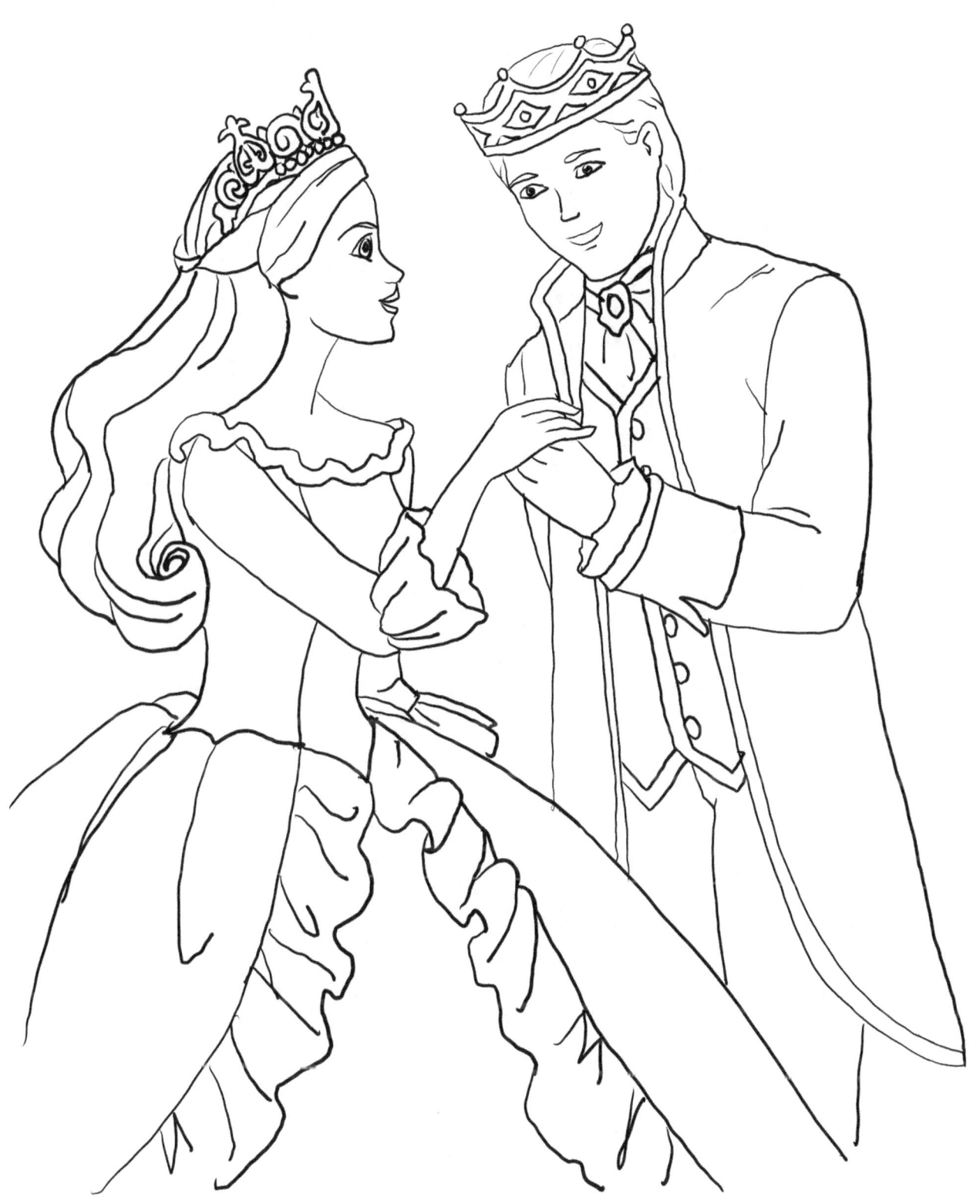

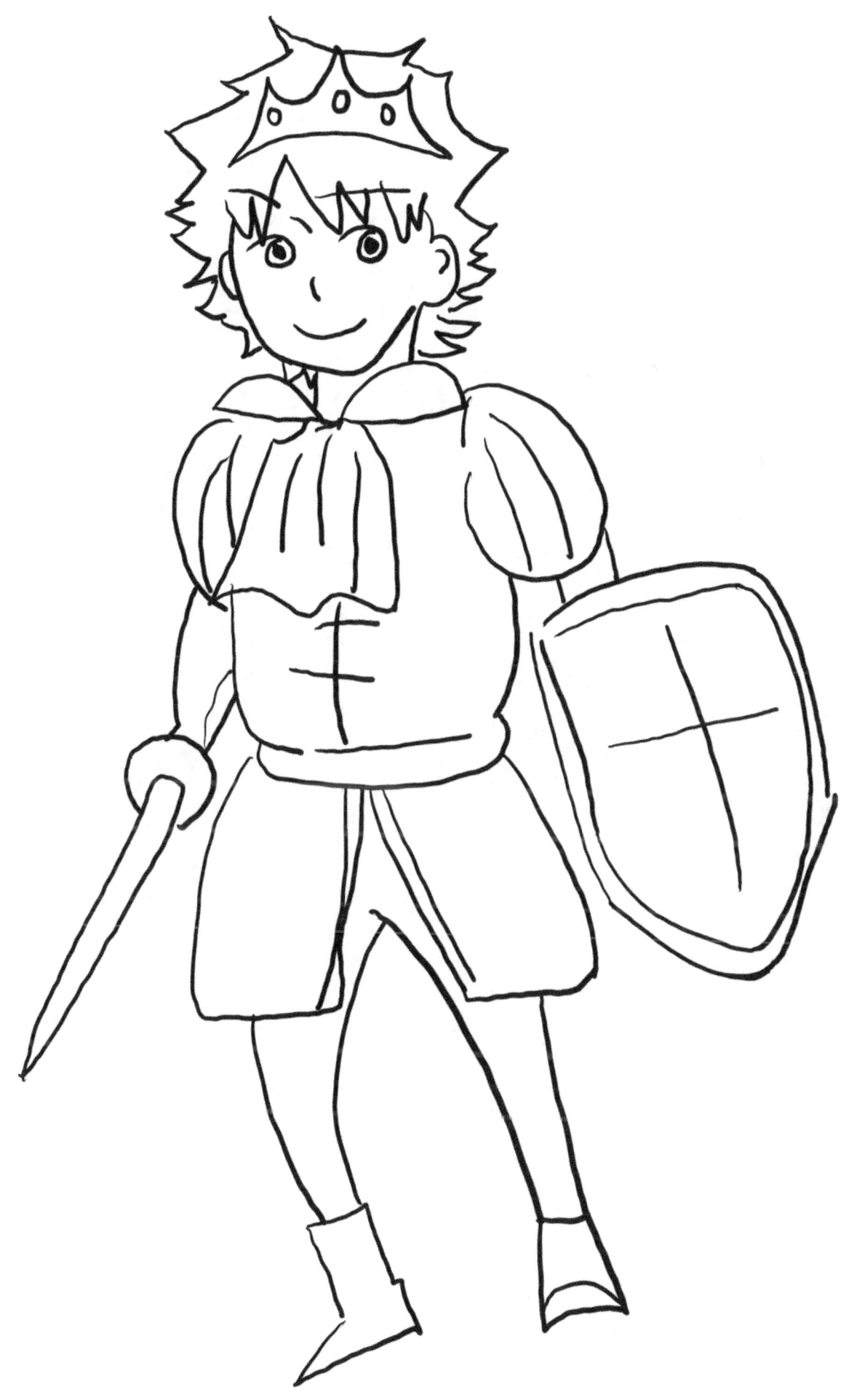

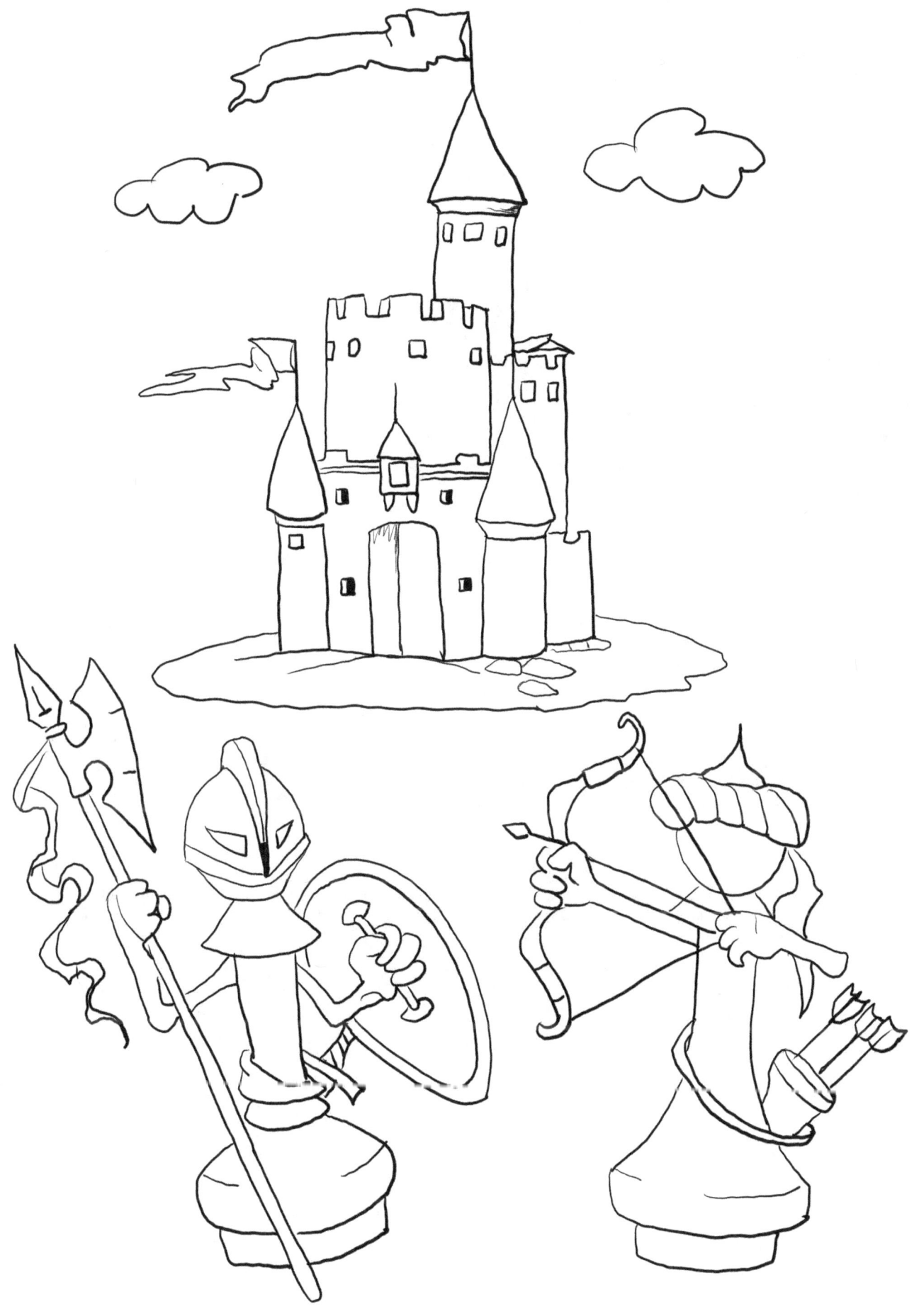

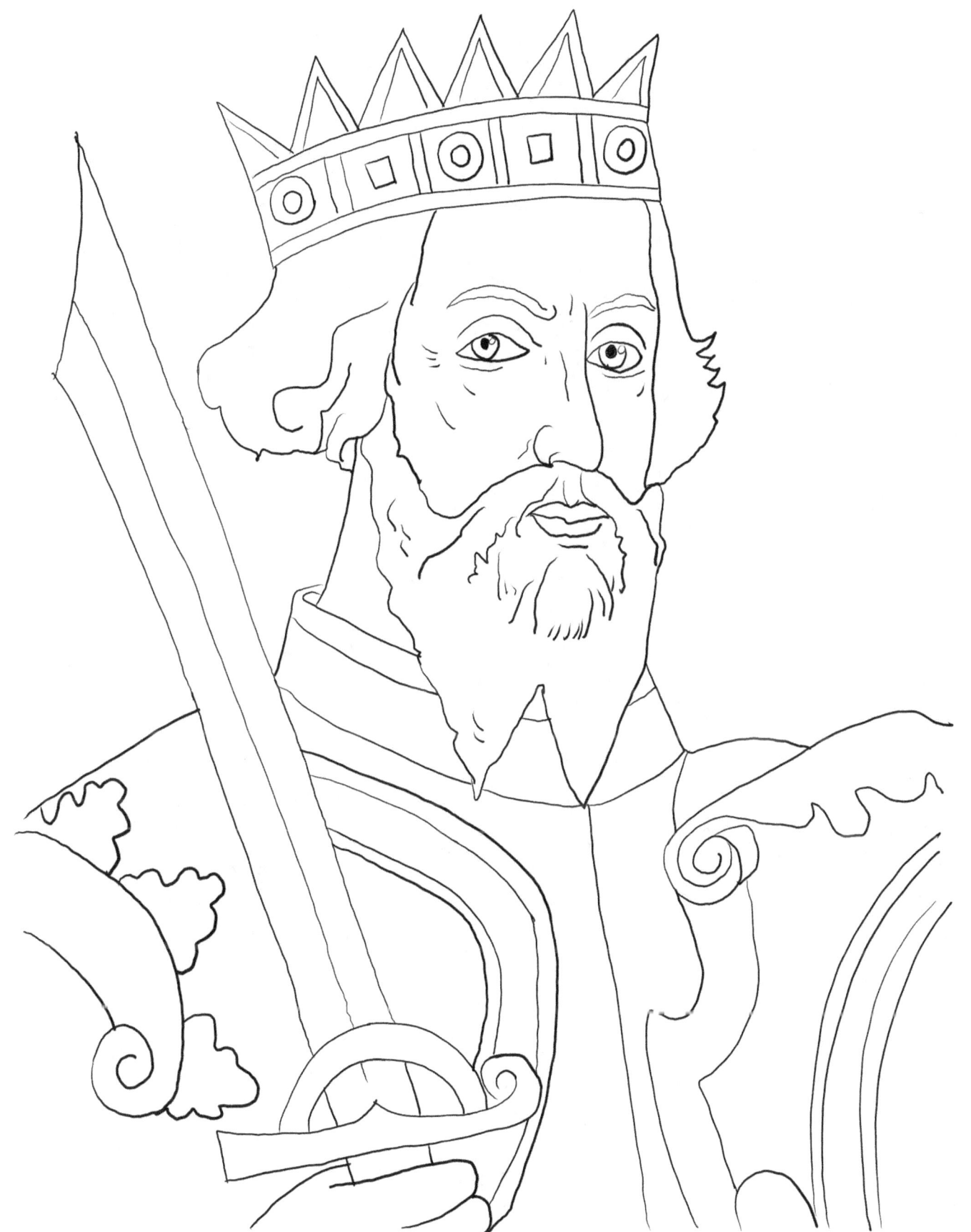

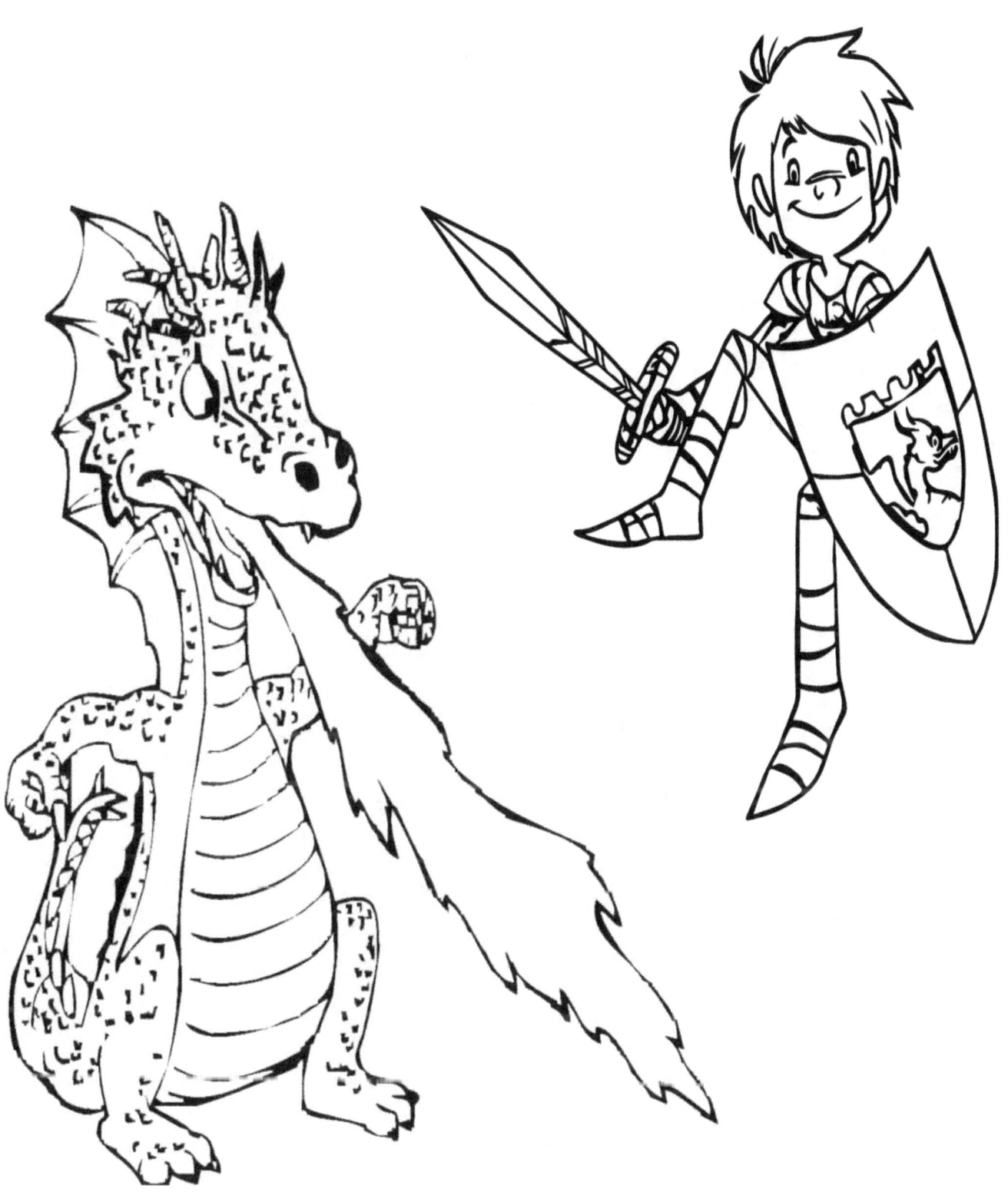

www.ingramcontent.com/pod-product-compliance
Lightning Source LLC
Chambersburg PA
CBHW082148230526
45467CB00043B/2412